THE COMPLETE

color

directory

THE COMPLETE

color

directory

A GUIDE TO USING COLOR IN YOUR HOME

ALICE WESTGATE

RAINCOAST BOOKS

Vancouver

First published in Canada in 1999 by

RAINCOAST BOOKS

8680 Cambie Street

Vancouver, B.C.

V6P 6M9

(604) 323-7100

www.raincoast.com

ISBN 1-55192-255-X

Canadian Cataloguing in Publication Data

Westgate, Alice.

Complete colour directory

1. Color in interior decoration. I. Title.

NK2115.5.C6W47 1999 747'.94 C99-910202-8

Reproduction and printing in Hong Kong by
Hong Kong Graphic and Printing Ltd.

This book was conceived, designed,
and produced by

THE IVY PRESS LIMITED

Art Director: PETER BRIDGEWATER

Senior Designer: CLARE BARBER

Designer: JANE LANAWAY

DTP Designer: CHRIS LANAWAY

Editorial Director: SOPHIE COLLINS

Managing Editor: ANNE TOWNLEY

Senior Project Editor: ROWAN DAVIES

Studio Photography: GUY RYECART

Collages: PIP ADAMS

Picture Researcher: VANESSA FLETCHER

This book is typeset in 9/16 Gill Sans Light

contents

how this book works

WALK INTO A HOME IMPROVEMENT STORE, browse through an interior design magazine, or visit a home decorating shop and you'll be bombarded with fantastic ways to color your home—vibrant shades, bold combinations, unusual textures, daring applications. You might love them and admire them, yet when it comes to choosing paint colors for your own surroundings you suddenly lose confidence and reach for the time-honored, easy-on-the-eye neutral shades that you've always chosen.

If you follow a few simple design rules you can fill any room with glorious color.

A yen for lime green still lies at the back of your mind, but something stops you—and that's a shame, because if it made your heart sing when you saw it in that store window or on the page of that magazine, chances are it will do the same in your living room. There's no quicker, easier, cheaper, or more flexible way to change the look of your home and the way you feel about living there, than by opening a can of paint, and there are no big secrets about using exciting colors to fabulous effect, at least not now that you've bought this book.

It's a myth to say that some people are born with an innate sense of color while others are not. The truth of the matter is that everyone has an emotional response to color because we all know what we like and dislike; choosing paints and fabrics is just a question of harnessing that reaction, calling it your own personal sense of style, and accepting that it is just as valid as any designer's taste.

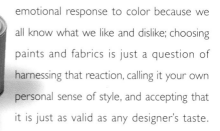

Inspirational photographs

Color tab dividers

Clear, helpful text

Perforated color swatches

This book will help you find your favorites and understand why they strike a chord within you. It will encourage you to mix your own paints, not only so you can enjoy working with the raw materials of color but also so you can achieve exactly the right look in the end.

The next few pages contain all the background information you'll need to get started, from understanding the color wheel to making your own colorboard, learning about light, tone, and texture along the way. The color-coded tabbed chapters that follow allow you to revel in every shade under the sun, exploring their appeal in a variety of ways, and gleaning inspiration from all manner of sources—from the natural world and historical trends to real-life homes, feng shui, and color therapy. Then you'll be ready to use the special, tear-out swatches to choose the right shade from each color family and combine it with the other decorative elements in your room scheme. The results will be fun, uplifting, creative, and individual. So put on your overalls—it's time to enrich your life with color.

use colors with similar tones for harmony

use contrasting colors to set one another off

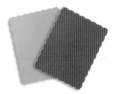

use complementary colors for strong impact

color theory

Decorating with color is about taste, experience, and experimentation. But while there's much to be said for just following your instincts, it does help to be a little scientific now and then, especially if you're weaning yourself off neutrals for the first time.

Cast your mind back to school science classes and you'll recall that white light is composed of many colors that can be seen individually when a beam is passed through a prism. The colors of the rainbow separate because each color has a different wavelength: red has the longest wavelength and the slowest frequency, violet the shortest wavelength and the fastest frequency. The reason we perceive something as, say, blue, is that the surface of the object on which the light falls absorbs all but the blue light waves, which are then reflected back to our eyes. The understanding that light is energy, and that different colors therefore have different energies, is central to practices such as color therapy and feng shui, which use color in many ways to enhance well-being.

White light separates into its constituent colors when it passes through a prism.

The color wheel allows you to see how all the colors in the spectrum work together; complementary colors are found opposite one another, while harmonious colors sit side by side.

The colors in this visible spectrum, produced by the separation of light according to wavelength, are traditionally joined end to end and shown as a color wheel—an important tool for decorators because it illustrates how colors relate to one another and what effect they will have on our surroundings. Colors that are adjacent are referred to as harmonious; colors that are opposite form a stark contrast and are described as complementary. If you're not sure whether two colors will go together, or if you're trying to work out how to improve a color scheme, the color wheel will probably provide the answer.

When thinking about color it is useful to understand the term "tone," which refers to a color's intensity: how light or dark a color is. Two different colors can have the same degree of intensity and, therefore, the same tone. A paint's tone can be altered by adding black, in which case it is called a shade—a darker version of the original—or by adding white, when it becomes a tint—a lighter version of the original. Assessing tones is crucial when combining two or more colors in a room since tonal values need to be similar for colors to balance successfully (see p. 18).

ochre

egg yolk

lemon

Buy sample paint cans and dab small areas on to your wall to judge a shade accurately.

(see p. 18)

CHOOSING COLORS

To help you choose a color, first answer these questions:

- which colors naturally appeal to you?
- which colors make you feel relaxed and which seem to give you energy?
- will the room be used for work, play, or relaxation?
- are you inspired by any colors in nature or a particular era in history?
- how much natural light does the room get?
- does the room face north, south, east, or west?
- do you want to make the space feel enclosing or open?

Taking your answers into consideration, use the following pages to assess which color meets your criteria the best.

color families

There are various ways of grouping colors, some based on color theory, others on aesthetics. It's useful to look at the groups and identify the ones that you are drawn to. You might decide to decorate all the rooms in your home with colors from the same family, to give a coherent look, or you may choose several according to the way in which the room will be used. For example, you might opt for cool, restful pastel shades in your bedroom or primaries for a child's playroom.

Notice your response to each of the following groups. Which make you feel calm and which give a sense of energy? Do you equate warm colors with coziness or oppression? Do cool shades make you feel relaxed or chilly? Go with your gut reactions and the colors you choose will serve you well.

A room decorated in a pastel palette includes a range of closely related yet subdued colors that blend well together and appear restful.

A room decorated in primary colors is perfect for areas of the house where you'd like to promote a sense of energy and vitality.

PRIMARY COLORS

Red, yellow, and blue are the three primary colors—so-called because you can't mix them from any other colors and because they are the colors from which all others are derived. Decorating in primaries gives bold, fun results and they are most appropriate for rooms where you would like to promote activity and learning.

SECONDARY AND TERTIARY COLORS

Mixing together two primary colors gives rise to the secondary colors—orange, green, and violet. Mixing any two secondaries gives a tertiary color (there are six of these altogether), and so on—each successive mixing creating colors that are less and less vivid and more and more subtle.

COMPLEMENTARY COLORS

Complementary colors sit opposite each other on the color wheel—matching tones of red and green, blue and orange, and yellow and purple—and have a zingy effect when seen together. Complementaries should be used as accent colors—an orange cushion on a blue sofa—to bring the room alive.

red

yellow

blue

orange (red and yellow)

green (blue and yellow)

violet (red and blue)

yellow

lilac

11

PASTEL COLORS

Powder blue, rose pink, and lemon yellow are all colors to which lots of white has been added. While pastels are light, bright, and undemanding—perfect for creating calm and serene schemes throughout the house—too many of them, or too pale a tint, can look insipid.

WARM AND COOL COLORS

The colors that appear beside red, orange, and yellow on the color wheel are warm, while the ones beside blue and violet are cool. However, clever mixing can modify them. Green, for example, heats up with the addition of yellow and cools down when mixed with blue, so it is important to know which version you prefer.

ADVANCING AND RECEDING COLORS

Warm colors advance and cool colors recede—a wall painted in a warm color appears to be closer to you than a wall painted in a cool color. Use this knowledge to play tricks with a room's proportions—paint a small room blue to push the walls back, or paint a large room red to warm it and give it a sense of intimacy.

powder blue

rose pink

tan t

hot

cold

rece

advancing

BLACK AND WHITE

Although they are not, strictly speaking, colors, black and white are nevertheless very useful as mixers when creating tints and shades (see p. 9)—that is, altering a color's tone to make it either lighter or darker. Myriad varieties of white paints are now available as alternatives to the bluey harshness of brilliant white, and these can also be used in their own right to create wonderfully pure, simple schemes. Monochrome color schemes are based on various tones of a single color. Opting for a monochrome look also cuts down what can sometimes seem like a limitless range of options.

NEUTRALS

This group includes shades such as cream, buff, and gray. "Neutral" is something of an umbrella term for colors that are naturally subdued and which echo the shades of natural materials such as earth and stone. They don't strike you as being either warm or cool immediately (although there is, of course, such a thing as a cool gray and a warm gray) so they play an important role in balancing, diluting, and setting off bright colors. What's more, they are blissfully easy to match with each other.

black

white

buff

cream

gray

color and light

tungsten bulbs give a slightly yellow light

spotlights give concentrated bursts of white light

full spectrum lighting mimics daylight

halogen lighting gives white light and saves energy

energy-saving fluorescent bulbs give flat, cold light

One of the most difficult aspects of choosing the right paint color is knowing how it will behave in different lights, and, unfortunately, it is an area that is often ignored. Any change in the level or quality of light in a room will alter the way we perceive the colors used in it. A specific color that looked great on a chart in your local paint store under a fluorescent bulb, will seem altogether different in a sunny kitchen and different again in a dark hallway. So it is vitally important that you take the time to check out all the possibilities, before you commit.

To do this, choose a sample–sized can of the desired color paint and use it to paint a large piece of cardboard or paper that can be moved around and attached to different areas of a wall. See how it looks in a dark corner of the room, as well as on a sunny wall, since shadows can make some colors seem incredibly gloomy. Check it out in natural light at different times of the day too, and compare the effect of weak morning rays to that of the warm evening sun, or cloudy days. Finally, see how the color changes in different types of artificial light. Common tungsten light bulbs cast a yellowish tinge over everything, making blues seem green and whites appear grubby, while fluorescent bulbs wash everything in cold, harsh blue. The good news is that the interplay between light and color can be used to

Pools of light created by spotlights are gentler than a single light source.

Ordinary light bulbs cast a yellow hue while fluorescent bulbs give a harsh, bluish edge.

The quality of natural light depends on the time of day, season, weather, and exposure of the room.

Candlelight gives a lovely glowing light that is perfect for relaxing evenings.

the decorator's advantage, compensating for less-than-perfect conditions. Choose colors that appear to alter and improve your existing light system, or the natural light that you have no control over. For example, if you're faced with decorating a cold, dingy, north-facing room, choose warm colors and you'll improve the light quality in an instant. Conversely, a busy kitchen filled with blazing morning sun can be pacified with cool blues or greens.

Choose lighting that is aesthetically pleasing as well as practical.

dragging brush: gives the paint a soft, lined effect

sponge: creates a subtle, speckled pattern

rocker: used to achieve a faux wood grain

rag: results in an uneven paint finish

steel wool: useful for creating an antique look

color and texture

The appearance of light—and therefore color—can vary according to the texture of the surface it is covering. So, when planning your color schemes, bear in mind that shiny surfaces reflect light and make colors appear more intense, whereas matte surfaces absorb light, making them seem paler.

A room is generally considered to be balanced if it contains a variety of textures in fabrics and on flooring as well as on the walls. Like many of the so-called rules of decorating, however, you can turn this principle upside down and combine similar textures in a room on purpose, giving a wonderful sense of simplicity and refinement. Look at your colorboard (see p. 19) to see whether the decorative elements you have chosen give the effect you would like.

Your first consideration when combining color with texture should be the finish of your paint. To create a matte finish look for whitewash, flat oil, casein, and matte latex paint. For shiny finishes think about acrylics, glazes, varnishes, and gloss paints. Midway between the two are such soft-sheen finishes as eggshell and vinyl silk.

It may be that a surface you plan to paint is already textured. If not, you can add texture—or give the impression of texture—by applying paint in a variety of ways.

COLORWASHING: *a subtly broken, multitoned texture created when layers of glaze are applied using brush strokes in different directions.*

DRAGGING: *a soft, lined effect achieved by drawing a special dragging brush through a surface glaze.*

STIPPLING: *a subtly grained surface texture created by hitting a glaze coat with a special stippling brush.*

RAGGING: *a distressed effect gained by dabbing a coat of glaze with a rag to reveal patches of base color.*

ANTIQUING: *a "time-worn" simulation created by removing some of the surface color with steel wool or sandpaper.*

SPONGING: *a speckled effect achieved when paint is applied using a sponge so that the base color can be seen through its open texture.*

GRAINING: *a faux wood treatment created by pulling a special rocker through a surface glaze to simulate the pattern of the grain.*

Quite apart from painted surfaces, remember that you can also vary or unify the quality of a room's textural interest by introducing new elements to your room scheme. These could be anything from knotty natural flooring, rough-hewn stone, and raw linens to smooth ceramic tiles, shimmering silks, or sleek laminates. They'll add depth and rich variety, making the whole scheme come alive.

members of the same
color family match well

a combination of blues
can sometimes seem cold

adjacent color families
make for a harmonious mix

combine color families
by matching similar tones

closely related colors make
pleasing combinations

matching colors

Deciding on the basic color for a room is perhaps the easiest part, because it is the most intuitive. And mixing it with darker or lighter shades of the same color is easy, too—just look down a color chart and you'll see that primrose and egg-yolk yellow look good together, as do sky blue and navy. But successfully combining one color with a completely different one is slightly more tricky—unless, that is, you know the golden rule about tone.

First, try to forget old sayings like "blue with green should never be seen." A glance at an interior designer's portfolio will prove that schemes based on these forbidden colors can work perfectly well. This is because the harmonious room scheme is the result of bringing together colors that have a similar tone—similar intensities of light or dark. Virtually any combination of colors will work as long as they have the same intensity.

So how can you tell if two colors have the same tone? Think about a black-and-white photograph: tone is what enables it to convey shape, depth, and perspective. The more intense tones appear as dark grays and black, while less intense ones are expressed in pale grays and white.

Try looking at a series of colors through half-closed eyes and you'll get a similar impression of which colors share a common tonal value. If you're new to decorating with lots of color, it will be very helpful to make up a colorboard which will allow

you to see how all the elements you are planning to use will work together. You'll need a square of cardboard or something similar onto which you can pin, staple, or stick swatches of fabric, dabs of paint, and samples of carpet, labeling them "walls," "woodwork," or "curtains" as you go. Start with a brush stroke of your base color. Then decide whether you want to go for harmony, in which case add blobs of paint that are shades or tints of that color; or whether you'd like to introduce a contrasting color, in which case add a stroke of a different color that has the same tone as your base color. Don't worry about making mistakes. If anything looks wrong, simply paint over it and try something else.

Putting together a colorboard lets you see how the colors you have in mind will work together. Include swatches of fabric and wallpaper, plus samples of paint and flooring.

If your room scheme needs a lift, try including an accessory in a complementary shade.

Next, build up fabrics and floorcoverings, remembering to incorporate things you aren't planning to change—maybe an existing carpet or furnishing fabric. Remember to keep an eye on the tonal relationships as you go. Then play around with accessories; if the whole thing needs a lift, look back at the color wheel (see p. 8), choose the appropriate complementary color, and add it as an accent—maybe a painted chair or a colored throw. Your colorboard and your understanding of color theory will allow you to be as subtle as you like or as bold as you dare. It really is your decision.

color and well-being

Because each color has its own vibrational energy, and because energy affects every cell in your body, there are many ways in which color can be used therapeutically to improve mood, emotions, and sometimes even health. You might already use color in this way, on a subconscious level, by wearing bright colors to boost your mood or cool ones to calm you down. Your choices may be based on cultural tradition (white symbolizes purity in some cultures, death in others) or could be purely symbolic (we talk about feeling green with envy or seeing red), but they might also be affected by the centuries of tradition and ancient schools of thought that see color as a way of healing and balancing mind and body.

COLOR AND FENG SHUI

Feng shui is the ancient Chinese art of placement—a way of arranging your living space in order to bring about balance and well-being in everything that you do. It is based on the premise that spiritual and physical health can only exist where the flow of energy—chi—is good; blocked or stagnant energy creates stress and illness. So the more vibrant and

THE FIVE ELEMENTS

- Earth—yellow, brown, orange—wholeness, unity
- Metal—white, gold, silver—children, leadership
- Water—black, blue, purple—career, power, knowledge
- Wood—green—family, good health, life
- Fire—red—passion, wealth and money, energy

energetic the colors you choose for your house, the more the energy will flow—that's good news for those who love vibrant surroundings. Also central to feng shui is the idea that all life is built upon five elements—earth, metal, water, wood, and fire. Each of these elements is associated with certain qualities of our existence and with certain colors; enhancing that color nurtures that element and brings all those qualities into your life.

THE COLORS OF YOUR BODY

The vibrational energy of each color in the spectrum is thought to promote good health in a corresponding area of the body:

- Red—kidneys
- Orange—reproductive system
- Yellow—pancreas, spleen, gall bladder
- Green—heart, lungs
- Blue—throat, thyroid
- Indigo—pituitary, ears, eyes, nose
- Violet—brain, nervous system

COLOR THERAPY

Color therapists believe that the energy in certain organs of the body corresponds to the energy of certain colors, and that these colors can be seen around us as our aura. Practitioners help alleviate physical or emotional illness—which result from an imbalance in energy—simply using color to reintroduce the correct vibrations. There are a number of ways to do this: you can use colored light; you can take a bath in colored water; you can eat certain foods; you can wear certain crystals; or you can visualize color during meditation.

If you, too, believe that color has the power to heal or bring about change, the way you decorate your home becomes more than just a matter of aesthetics; the colors you choose can heal and nurture you, making your living space something of a sanctuary from the stresses of the world.

tourmaline

lapis lazuli

amber

amethyst

mixing your own paint

You can buy paint in just about every color under the sun at home improvement stores. Some shades are available off the shelf, others are mixed for you there, but all will give you tremendous scope to use a host of colors in a multitude of ways. If this book has inspired you to experiment, commercial paints will certainly give you plenty of choices. However, as an alternative to these mass-produced products, many people like to get back to basics and mix their own paints using the traditional materials and formulas that have been employed for centuries, handed down through generations of craftspeople.

Mixing your own paints gives you the satisfaction of working with color in its raw form.

WHY MIX YOUR OWN PAINTS?

It can be incredibly satisfying to work with color in its raw form and to see how a basic pigment such as iron oxide, for example, creates a varnish the color of ox blood; or to see how an ultramarine blue pigment shines out of an old-fashioned powder-blue casein paint. Some people prefer to mix their own natural paints because these products contain no petrochemicals and are therefore

SAFETY

As with many decorating materials, some of the pigments, paints, and oil-based materials in the recipes featured in this book need to be handled with care. Where particular caution is required, it will be highlighted in the recipe method. It is always a good idea, however, to wear a dust mask and protective gloves when handling the materials. Don't eat, drink, or smoke when working with pigments; don't inhale the dust; avoid contact with the eyes; and ensure that your working space is adequately ventilated. Always follow any safety instructions given on the label.

considered more environmentally friendly. They also find that mixing a paint from scratch is far more flexible than using something from a manufacturer, because the depth and intensity of the color can easily be altered simply by adding more or less pigment.

You'll find that as you attempt more and more paint recipes, you will build up an ever-increasing stock of basic paint pigments. Once you are familiar with the traditional methods by which these can be combined and applied, your paint library will inspire you to create your own recipes and devise still more ways to introduce color into your home.

FOLLOWING THE PAINT RECIPES

Recipes accompany each tabbed section in this book, revealing how a selection of natural pigments from a color family can be used to create a variety of different paint finishes, from colorwashes and glazes for walls to stains for furniture and liming waxes for floorboards. All the recipes are graded according to difficulty, so you can gauge the complexity of the techniques involved before you begin. Detailed instructions are given at every step, and there's plenty of advice on the areas of the home that would be most suitable for each technique. All the recipes can be attempted without any previous experience of mixing paint; you should feel able to just roll up your sleeves and get started.

cobalt violet

indigo

green

yellow

Remember to follow the safety instructions that accompany the recipes and are specified by the products that you use. A dust mask should always be worn when dealing with powder pigments, and bear in mind that oil-based products such as beeswax or varnishes are flammable.

WHAT YOU WILL NEED

Buy the raw materials—such as pigments and mediums—from a specialized paint supplier (see List of Suppliers p. 190). Materials such as rags, brushes, sponges, and steel wool, for example, are all readily available from the usual retail outlets.

POINTS TO REMEMBER

Bear in mind that when mixing your own paints you will often be dealing with natural rather than man-made materials, which may vary slightly in color from one batch to the next. So there are no guarantees that your painted surfaces will look exactly like the ones illustrated.

Paint pigments are a limited natural resource, and the precise color mined from one geological strata will be different from that extracted from another. Many people believe that this precious quality gives natural paints even more appeal, and are prepared to sacrifice a little uniformity and predictability in return for the knowledge that there is something unique about the colors they have made.

Hand-mixed paints allow you to experiment with different shades and finishes.

EQUIPMENT

- Dust mask
- Small brush
- Large brush
- Dragging brush
- Stippling brush
- Paint tray
- Sponges
- Rags
- Sandpaper
- Steel wool

QUICK GUIDE TO MATERIALS

linseed oil varnish

CASEIN MILK PAINT (DISTEMPER): a traditional white paint containing casein (a milk derivative) and chalks. Does not flake or rub off like chalk paints or whitewashes. Can be used on its own or colored with pigments.

BEESWAX-BASED FURNITURE WAX: a traditional nontoxic protective surface for floors and furniture. Adding white pigment creates a liming wax.

CITRUS PEEL OIL THINNER: a natural alternative to chemical-based solvents..

crackle glaze

LATEX GLAZING LIQUID: mixed with pigments to aid the application of a colorwash.

CRACKLE GLAZE: creates an aged surface effect. Applied between two different colored paints, it causes the top layer to crack as it dries—this reveals flashes of the base color underneath.

FLAT LATEX PAINT: paint with an opaque, uniform finish, and no shine whatsoever.

casein milk paint

LINSEED OIL VARNISH: a natural alternative to conventional varnishes. Hard-wearing gloss finish.

METALLIC POWDER: gold, silver, or bronze powder pigments give a metallic finish when mixed with other carriers such as varnish or emulsion.

bronze metallic powder

PIGMENTS: derived from earth and rock, and supplied as powders. Used in paint, varnishes, and glazes. Give a depth of color and reflect light more softly than chemically made colors.

TRANSPARENT OIL GLAZE: a varnish that creates a light, clear finish for woodwork. Adding pigments makes a colored stain or glaze.

key to recipe symbols

Our paint recipes demonstrate a wide range of applications and techniques that will make varying demands on your time, skill, and wallet. These icons should help you to decide which recipes are appropriate for you.

DEPTH OF COLOR

This is a measure of how strong the paint color will be once you have allowed it to dry. Colors are usually darker when wet.

 will provide a very strong, rich, deep color that won't fade much over time

 will provide a reasonably rich, strong color, but not a very dark one

 will provide a rather pale finish without much depth of color

DURABILITY

Measures the hardiness of a particular finish or color. Decorative effects are frequently less hard-wearing than plain ones.

 will provide a tough, hard-wearing finish suitable for busy areas of the house

 will provide a fairly hard-wearing finish but won't take too much punishment

 will provide a delicate, fragile finish that needs to be protected from knocks

DIFFICULTY

Gives an indication of how much skill and experience will be required to execute the recipe correctly.

 very easy to make and apply, suitable for a beginner

 rather easy to make and apply, suitable for a beginner or someone with a little skill

quite easy to make and apply but will require some skill and experience

quite difficult to make and apply and will require a fair amount of skill

very difficult to make and apply and will require a lot of skill and experience

TIME REQUIRED

This measures the amount of time that will be required to make up the recipe, apply all the coats, and allow them to dry.

 not very time-consuming; should be completed within half a day

 quite time-consuming; should be completed within a day

 very time consuming; will take a day or more to complete

GLOSSY OR MATTE

Measures the finish of the paint surface, whether glossy (shiny and reflective), matte (dull and non-reflective) or broken.

 will provide a high-sheen, glossy surface

 will provide a broken surface, glossy in parts and matte in parts

 will provide a non-reflective, matte surface

OPAQUE/TRANSLUCENT

Gives an indication of whether the color finish will be nontransparent and light-absorbing, or transparent and light-emitting.

 will provide an opaque, nontransparent, light-absorbing finish

 will provide a transparent, light-emitting finish

red

RED is a color for the brave and bold, for anyone who wants to bring heat, intensity, and passion to their surroundings. Yet while lavish swaths of red speak of drama, vitality, and energy, related shades such as soft candy pink and earthy terra-cotta provide gentler variations on the theme, making this color family incredibly versatile—the most powerful in the interior designer's palette.

inspirations

Spice shades inspire a rich
and vibrant decorating palette.

If you're worried about using red because it has associations with anger and passion that make it seem too daring and demanding, remember that shades of this color occur time and time again in the natural world, without ever appearing garish. Take inspiration from the reds you see in gardens, forests, and country landscapes and you'll begin to use related shades in ways that are striking but never strident.

The papery petals of poppies
might kindle an idea for a
room scheme based on soft
pinks or reds.

Notice how red berries shine out against a backdrop of foliage, and how the red of poisonous fungi alerts us to their presence on the forest floor; transfer this principle to your home and use the same bright, advancing shade to create eye-catching accents amid more subdued schemes. Look at a field of poppies or a scarlet pimpernel nestling in the grass and you'll see the zinging effect of complementary colors at work; both contrasts show just how powerful even a splash of bright red can be in a predominantly green room. Alternatively, go for subtler reds and use the shades of ripe apples, cherries, and raspberries as the basis for warming, mellow schemes; move toward the orange end of the spectrum, however, and you adopt the fiery hues of autumn leaves, sunsets, and glowing embers that give your home a sense of drama.

Look at the ground and you'll see why reds can also be among the earthiest of shades. For centuries colors such as terracotta have been an adornment staple because the earth pigments from which they were derived were inexpensive and easily available. In contrast, pure reds such as carmine, scarlet, crimson, and vermilion were rarer and therefore more expensive. These historic associations—red-browns in rustic settings and pure reds in opulent ones—are echoed in today's decorating schemes; russets are the mainstay of Shaker-style interiors, while vibrant crimsons fill many a luxurious dining room.

Turkish carpets make the most of hot reds, oranges, and golds. Together these colors bring warmth to an interior.

Rich reds can transport you around the globe—use them to give a sense of the exotic.

As well as the social conventions, various shades of red have strong associations with certain periods in history. Deep red combined with an exuberant pattern recreates the look of a Victorian parlor, while orange-red reminds us of the frescoes of ancient Egypt and Pompeii. Rose pink recreates the femininity of the early 18th-century boudoirs, while shocking pink harks back to its heyday in the 1930s.

Reds can also transport you to far-flung lands. Spice shades take you to India and Turkey, where rich reds adorn saris, kilims, and carpets; terracotta conjures up images of farmhouse style in Tuscany and Provence; and red lacquer delivers you to China, where it symbolizes luck and good fortune.

PLASTER-COLORED CASEIN

This popular color and finish recreates the look of freshly plastered walls. Instead of casein milk paint (distemper) you can use a natural flat latex paint without vinyl. This will require a larger quantity of pigment, and the finish will be more even and less rustic looking. Suitable for living rooms, bedrooms, and hallways.

INGREDIENTS

Coverage: approximately 48yds² (40m²)

- *5½oz (160g) alizarin crimson pigment*
- *1⅓ gallon (5 liters) water*
- *glass jar*
- *9lbs (4kg) casein milk paint (distemper)*
- *clean plastic bucket*
- *spoon*
- *small brush for edges*
- *large brush*

METHOD

■ Soak the pigment in enough water to cover overnight, making sure that all lumps have dissolved. Prepare the casein milk paint in the bucket according to the instructions, adding enough water to make a smooth thin paint. Prime an absorbent surface with a coat of raw casein milk paint. Add half of the pigment to your paint and stir thoroughly.

■ Working in a cool, ventilated room, apply samples to the wall. Add more pigment to the paint as desired. Paint the edges first using the small brush, then use the large brush and apply paint working from top to bottom and finishing one wall at a time. The translucent casein milk paint becomes opaque when dry. Allow the paint to dry completely before applying a second coat in the same way.

SAFETY: always wear a dust mask when handling pigments

BURNT SIENNA GLAZE

This light effect will soften stark white walls with the hue of morning sunlight. It is much loved in children's bedrooms, but goes equally well in halls and kitchens or any space which needs a "lift."

INGREDIENTS

Coverage: approximately 48yds² (40m²)

- 1¾oz (50g) burnt sienna pigment
- ¾–1 gallon (3–4 liters) water
- glass jar
- 1 quart (1 liter) clear latex glazing liquid
- clean plastic bucket
- spoon
- brush
- sponge (optional)
- rags

SAFETY: always wear a dust mask when handling pigments

METHOD

■ Cover the pigment in water and soak overnight, making sure that all lumps have dissolved. Add the prepared pigment to the glazing liquid in the bucket and add the rest of the water. Stir well until the ingredients are blended.

■ In a cool unheated room, practice applying the glaze with a brush or sponge on some paper. Use smooth round movements, keeping the glaze even. Make sure your surface is clean and dust-free and apply the glaze. Finish one wall at a time and use a rag to wipe away brush or sponge marks. Do not worry about neat edges but leave an uneven, natural edge.

■ This application will be translucent, leaving a veil of pigment on the walls. Allow the first coat to dry completely before deciding whether you want to apply more coats to strengthen the effect. For variety, you could apply a second or third layer over random areas, using rounded, organic strokes, reminiscent of cloud patterns.

OX-BLOOD RED WOOD VARNISH

Ox-blood red is a traditional color based on the common (and inexpensive) red oxide pigment. This recipe is for a hard-wearing, long-lasting treatment for interior or exterior wood, including floors.

INGREDIENTS

Coverage: approximately 22yds² (20m²)

- *8¾oz (250g) red oxide pigment*
- *½ gallon (2.5 liters) oil-based varnish*
- *⅓ cup (0.1 liters) turpentine or citrus peel oil thinner*
- *glass jar*
- *teaspoon*
- *spoon*
- *brush*
- *primer*

METHOD

■ Soak the pigment in a small quantity of varnish and the thinner overnight. Grind the pigment into the oils using the back of a teaspoon to create a smooth paste. When the pigment is completely lumpfree add it to the remaining varnish. Stir thoroughly until a rich red color is consistent throughout.

■ Make sure your wood is clean and dry and prime very dry or absorbent wood with a primer. In a ventilated area, apply the varnish systematically, using at least two coats for floors or exterior surfaces, allowing each coat to dry thoroughly before applying the next one.

SAFETY: always wear a dust mask when handling pigments and follow safety instructions when working with oil-based products

VIBRANT ORANGE AND TERRA-COTTA WASHES

*Suitable for living rooms, hallways and inspiring kitchens,
this broken color effect is sure to enliven your home.*

INGREDIENTS

Coverage: approximately 48yds² (40m²)

- 4½oz (130g) red ochre pigment
- approximately 1 quart (1 liter) water
- glass jar
- 1 gallon (5 liters) white latex paint
- clean plastic bucket
- 4 spoons
- roller or large brush
- 1½oz (40g) orange pigment
- ¾oz (20g) red oxide pigment
- 1 quart (1 liter) turpentine or citrus peel oil thinner
- 3 clean glass jars
- 3 teaspoons
- ⅔ gallon (2.5 liters) transparent oil glaze
- 3 large glass jars with lids
- brush
- rags

METHOD

- Soak 3½oz (100g) of red ochre pigment in about 1 quart of water overnight and mix in with the latex paint the next day. Apply to the walls.

- Divide the thinner into three and soak the remaining pigments, keeping each color separate, overnight. Break up lumps using the back of a teaspoon. Pour one-third of the oil glaze into each of the large glass jars. Add the larger part of each prepared pigment to the glaze and stir.

- In a ventilated room, practice using free brush strokes on paper. Add more pigment as necessary or add thinner if the glaze is too thick. Apply one color at a time to your walls, leaving each coat to dry thoroughly; possibly overnight. Start with the red ochre, then the orange and finally the red oxide glaze. Brush out the glaze, to avoid drips. Use rags to remove brush marks and apply glaze to the edges.

SAFETY: always wear a dust mask when handling pigments and follow safety instructions when working with oil-based products

healing with red

RED IN FENG SHUI

Red has the longest wavelength and in feng shui is associated with the element of fire, so using this color family in the home can make you feel more active and energetic. Painting the whole house red would certainly boost the flow of chi, but living amid such unremitting energy would ultimately be aggravating and stressful. So opt for touches of red, rusts, or pinks in certain rooms instead, particularly if you'd like to stimulate a fire within you—perhaps

BELOW *Add small areas of red to stimulate passion and increase your energy levels—a splash of paint or some well-chosen acccessories should do the job.*

A vase of red flowers will boost energy levels as you enter the house.

The color red is associated with the fire element; its presence encourages the beneficial flow of chi.

Introducing goldfish into a neutral-colored room will provide a counterbalance to any overpowering earth energy.

to find illumination at work or passion at home. A plant with red flowers, a red candle, or a tank containing goldfish would all be particularly auspicious.

RED IN COLOR THERAPY

Color therapists use red's warming, stimulating rays to soothe muscular aches and ease some circulatory disorders. If you're feeling short of energy it will pep you up; if you're feeling lonely it will make you more secure. Decorating your hallway red—and even painting your front door red—can promote these qualities throughout the home.

You are likely to be attracted to the red family if you are naturally talkative, full of life, quick-thinking, and perhaps even hotheaded, but it is not always advisable to surround yourself with reds if you already display these characteristics in abundance. Only you can tell whether painting your rooms in shades of red will enhance these high-energy qualities for the better and improve your health, or whether it would be too stimulating and—ultimately—too tiring.

RED AND YOUR HEALTH

Red can alleviate:	*Red can aggravate:*
■ head colds	■ anger
■ poor circulation	■ inflammation, fever, or infection
■ muscular disorders	
■ anemia	■ heart problems
■ lack of energy	■ insomnia
	■ high blood pressure

real life

Rich, vibrant reds create instant drama. Paint bold expanses of it for theatrical impact. Add pizzazz to any color scheme with splashes of red on cushions, vases, or rugs. Red lampshades will soften and warm a room by casting a cozy glow. Stimulating red contributes a buzz to any environment.

SPICY REDS are a good choice in this lofty living room because they add warmth to a space that could otherwise easily appear cold and unwelcoming. It is a real challenge to make grand rooms with high ceilings and large windows seem relaxed and intimate, but color alone overcomes the problem here—the fabrics used on the sofa and curtains, along with the abundance of wood on flooring and furniture, add plenty of heat.

A single splash of red may be enough to enliven a room, adding both welcome richness and warmth.

THIS CORNER has an almost shrinelike quality due to its harmonious, enveloping colors, the choice of artwork on the walls, and the quite unusual lamp that provides a focal point. Its decoration strikes a clever balance between relaxation and stimulation: the range of textures and patterns on the daybed invite repose, while the variety of reds, yellows, and browns assist in maintaining energy levels. Together, this produces a room that is the perfect place in which to sit during moments of reflection or inspiration.

Choose fabrics in related colors and use together to create a unified scheme.

Vivid Gerber Daisies complement rooms decorated in bright, Caribbean colors.

AREAS OF BRIGHT, Caribbean pink amid an expanse of pure white gives this atrium a tropical air; use this formula to give a similarly sun-drenched, summery feel to a house in cooler climes. Notice how the alcoves and door surrounds, which are painted in an advancing color, make the potentially sparse space seem more enclosed and cohesive. This effect is intensified because the few remaining decorative elements in the room—the upholstered chair and the ornamental plates—are also linked together by this strong, positive color.

A SOFT, DUSTY shade of duck-egg blue helps to create a rustic Shaker-style kitchen, complete with traditional peg rail, butler's sink, basketware, and tiled floor. To balance the blue of the cupboards, the walls are painted a rich cream, but it is the red tones of the terra-cotta floor and the wooden worktops that add another important element of color, intensifying the warmth of the room. All three colors are well-matched tonally, which gives the scheme an inherent sense of harmony.

The naturally red colors of terra-cotta tiles will introduce heat to any room.

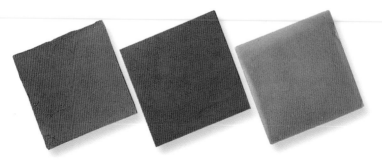

good combinations

Depending on the mood you intend to create, red can be combined with colors that either enhance or play down its warmth and vigor.

As long as their tones are equally matched there's nothing to stop you from teaming bright reds and pinks with turquoise, orange, and touches of lime for an explosion of color that can seem exotic in airy rooms and wonderfully jewel-like in enclosed ones. Soft sugar pinks, on the other hand, find natural partners with other pastel shades such as lemon, baby blue, and lavender.

Red forms the basis of some extremely sophisticated schemes when used with navy and forest green; softer versions use terra-cottas or paler plaster pinks, which have a natural affinity for denim blues and olive greens. Gold and red are traditional companions in opulent schemes—they're a favorite in dining rooms where candlelight enriches them beautifully.

Apple red and sage green gives a North American folk-art look and is also a time-honored combination in Swedish interiors, while red and white always gives a clean, jaunty look—useful for taking the heat out of this vibrant primary.

For warmth and intensity, combine red with yellow— it's a bold but cheerful mix.

Pale pink goes well with light shades of lemon, creating a soft and refreshing scheme.

White takes the heat out of bright primary red and balances its intensity.

Alongside the cooling influence of denim blue, pink will appear less saccharine.

Balancing the deep tones of terra cotta with olive green creates a pleasing palette.

Strong pinks look best beside similarly strident partners—lime green is a good choice here.

Navy and red is a classic color combination for interiors with a sophisticated air.

using red naturally

If you are still wary of using strong reds, remember that the naturally warm shades of terra-cotta and wood will create subtle red-based color combinations without any of the risks you might associate with using the bright, pure hues themselves. Red accessories are another safe option—bring in splashes of color here and there until you feel able to experiment on a larger scale.

yellow

UPLIFTING and uncompromisingly happy, yellow raises the spirits and brings a sense of joy wherever it is used. It is the brightest color in the spectrum, so your rooms will be light and vibrant even if you choose the most pure and intense yellow you can find. Whether you choose warm shades of deep saffron, cheery sunflower, and rich ochre, or cool tints of acid lemon, delicate primrose, and pale butter, all will fill your house with sunshine.

inspirations

If you're unsure of the effect yellow will have on a room, close your eyes and imagine some of the ways nature paints with yellow: the first daffodils of spring, clumps of delicate primroses peeping out of mossy green woodland, a carpet of buttercups, a field of towering sunflowers. All are powerful symbols of joy and life; all reflect the warm glow of the sun. Yellow is the color that will bring all of these qualities into your home. Your choice of shade—whether cool, warm, or acidic—might be inspired by anything from lemons piled high in a bowl and the jars of spices in your kitchen, to wonderful scenic vistas—an exotic sandy beach, a parched desert, or a field of ripening corn.

Let nature inspire your favorite shade—choose the warm tones of sunflowers and calendulas or the pale tints of primroses and narcissi.

Decorating ideas can spring from the most unlikely sources; yellow schemes might be ignited by the livery of a New York taxi or the paint finish of an abandoned truck.

While vibrant yellow is a useful accent color, adding splashes of warmth to a cool room and drawing the eye to detail, it is also a relatively easy color to use in large expanses on walls since it is light and bright enough to cope with any size room and any lighting condition. Yellow will enhance the appeal of a sunny room, as well as bring warmth and light to a cold, north-facing one, so it's a useful color to turn to when the natural light levels in a room are low.

If you're drawn to the warmer yellows in the spectrum, look to food as your inspiration: butter, egg yolks, yellow peppers, and golden plums. Consider also the rich, orangey hues of saffron. The color of this rare and expensive spice, derived from the stigmas of the crocus, is the source of many of the yellows we associate with the East, in particular the sacred color of the robes worn by Buddhist monks. Along with turmeric, mustard, and ochre, saffron presents the softer face of the yellow family and is a wonderful, uplifting way of bringing richness and warmth to any room in the house.

The Stonecutters (above) by Van Gogh illustrates the artist's continuing love affair with this color family. Saffron robes worn by Buddhist monks (below) emphasize the color's sacred associations.

The pure primary yellow we take for granted nowadays wasn't available to interior designers until the early part of the 19th century, when chrome yellow—a pigment obtained from lead chromates—first became widely available. Before that the decorator's palette was mainly derived from ochre and raw sienna which were warmer but less vibrant. The advent of this new yellow sparked off a decorating trend that we still associate with Empire style.

Artists such as Van Gogh and Monet were transfixed by yellow—the latter's radiant all-yellow dining room at his home in Giverny, France, is a wonderful expression of his love for the color. It has inspired many others to follow suit and create vibrant, sun-drenched rooms of their own.

yellow ochre

casein milk paint

SOFT OCHRE-COLORED CASEIN

This is a classic color and finish, proven to suit many different styles of interiors. Ideal for living rooms, bedrooms, and hallways.

INGREDIENTS

Coverage: approximately 48yds² (40m²)

- 1lb (500g) yellow ochre pigment
- 1 gallon (5 liters) water
- glass jar
- 9lb (4kg) casein milk paint (distemper)
- clean plastic bucket
- spoon
- small brush for edges
- large brush for covering

METHOD

■ Cover the pigment in water and soak overnight. Prepare the casein milk paint in a bucket according to the instructions, using the rest of the water. Prime an absorbent surface with a coat of uncolored milk paint. Add the prepared pigment to the paint and stir thoroughly until the paint has the consistency of whipping cream.

■ Working in a cool, ventilated room, paint the edges of the wall first using the small brush, then use the large brush and apply the milk paint systematically working from top to bottom, finishing one wall at a time. The translucent milk paint becomes opaque when dry. Allow one coat to dry completely before applying another one.

SAFETY: always wear a dust mask when handling pigments

RAW SIENNA VEIL GLAZE

Suitable for bathrooms, kitchens, halls, and stairways, this glaze produces a hard-wearing washable surface with a broken color effect. The glaze can be applied to painted walls and wooden surfaces treated with eggshell or gloss paint and sanded to provide a key. Raw sienna veil glaze works best over white.

INGREDIENTS

Coverage: approximately 12yds² (10m²)

- ¾oz (20g) raw sienna pigment
- 2 cups (.5 liter) turpentine or citrus peel oil thinner
- glass jar
- teaspoon
- 1 quart (1 liter) transparent oil glaze
- spoon
- large glass jar with lid
- brush
- rags

METHOD

■ Soak the pigment in enough thinner to cover overnight. Break up any lumps using the back of a teaspoon to create a smooth paste. Stir the oil glaze well and pour into a large sealable glass jar. Add the prepared pigment and stir well. Then stir in the remaining thinner.

■ In a well-ventilated room, apply some sample brush strokes in an unobtrusive corner, practicing the application. Brush out the glaze well, so you don't get drips and runs. Apply more layers when the previous coat is completely dry. To create a richly textured effect, dab a rag of loosely woven fabric into glaze while it is still wet.

SAFETY: always wear a dust mask when handling pigments and follow safety instructions when working with oil-based products

PRIMARY YELLOW WALLS

Primary yellow walls go well with modern interiors and are extremely cheerful and sunny. Eminently suitable for children's rooms and modern living rooms, or as a feature within an ethnically inspired interior, this paint is best applied over white painted walls.

INGREDIENTS

Coverage: approximately 48yds² (40m²)

- *3⅓lbs (1.5kg) yellow pigment*
- *3 quarts (3 liters) water*
- *glass jar*
- *6½lbs (3kg) casein milk paint (distemper)*
- *clean plastic bucket*
- *spoon*
- *small brush for edges*
- *large brush for covering*

METHOD

■ Soak the pigment in enough water to cover overnight, making sure any lumps are dissolved. Prepare the casein milk paint in a bucket according to the instructions, using the remaining water. Add the prepared pigment and stir thoroughly.

■ In a cool, ventilated room, apply the paint. Use a small brush at the edges first and work systematically, finishing one wall at a time. You will need to apply two coats, but always let the first coat dry completely before applying the next.

SAFETY: always wear a dust mask when handling pigments

yellow ochre

turpentine

linseed oil varnish

YELLOW WOOD STAIN

This is a bright and upbeat stain for all light woods and can be used on furniture, built-in units and woodwork. Suitable for a child's bedroom, hall, stairwell, or to brighten up a kitchen.

INGREDIENTS

Coverage: approximately 12yds² (10m²)

- *8¾ oz (250g) yellow ochre pigment*
- *⅓ cup (0.1 liter) turpentine or citrus peel oil thinner*
- *glass jar*
- *teaspoon*
- *2 cups (.5 liter) linseed oil varnish*
- *large glass jar with lid*
- *spoon*
- *brush*

METHOD

■ Soak the pigment in the thinner overnight. Grind the pigment with the back of a teaspoon to create a smooth, lumpfree paste. Transfer the varnish to a sealable glass jar and add the prepared pigment, stirring thoroughly.

■ Before application make sure your wood is clean and dry. Do not prime the wood. In a well-ventilated room apply the stain with a brush, working it into the wood where necessary. Apply one coat only for interior use, and three coats for a weatherproof finish to exterior wood, allowing each coat to dry thoroughly before applying the next one.

SAFETY: always wear a dust mask when handling pigments and follow safety instructions when working with oil-based products

healing
with yellow

YELLOW IN FENG SHUI

Yellow is vibrant and full of positive energy, so light, bright shades on walls will help the life-giving forces to flow and give rise to an overall sense of freshness and vitality. This color is associated with the earth element and with a sense of unity and wholeness, so it should be introduced to your surroundings if your health needs boosting or your mind needs balancing. Objects made from natural materials—such as a piece of earthenware pottery or a sculpture

BELOW *Paint your kitchen yellow and its positive energy can be shared by everyone who uses it.*

Yellow is a good color choice in family rooms because it promotes harmonious relationships.

Enhance the wholesome earth energy that is associated with yellow by introducing a ceramic vase filled with sunflowers.

If a yellow room seems too stimulating, balance it with cooling shades of blue.

Yellow makes a room seem instantly welcoming, a characteristic that should be reflected in your choice of furniture.

made of china or plaster—also help restore this state of equilibrium, especially in the presence of yellow. A ceramic vase filled with sunflowers would therefore give you optimum benefit.

Yellow in a room also promotes a sense of well-being and harmony among those who regularly use the space, so it is a good choice for a family room such as the living room or kitchen.

YELLOW IN COLOR THERAPY

As the color of the sun, yellow's most obvious therapeutic value comes from its ability to raise the spirits and inject vitality—avoid using bright yellow in rooms where peace and relaxation are your priority, the bedroom or bathroom for example. Yellow also has a beneficial effect on mental activity, focusing the mind, sharpening thought processes, increasing concentration, and improving the memory, so it is an excellent choice for a study or workroom.

This color family is also therapeutic in kitchens where it nourishes the digestive system, stimulating, cleansing, and reviving your whole body.

YELLOW AND YOUR HEALTH

Yellow can alleviate:
- depression
- jaundice
- fatigue
- digestive problems
- mental strain

Yellow can aggravate:
- hyperactivity
- fear
- insomnia
- jealousy
- aggression

real life

Yellow can be warm, glowing, and golden; it also contributes cooler, gentle shades such as primrose. Sharp, citrus lemon adds punch, especially if combined with acidic green or bright turquoise. If natural light levels are low, a shade such as egg-yolk yellow maintains warmth and freshness.

Accessorize a yellow kitchen with coordinating glass and tableware to bring yet more sunshine into the room.

HAPPY SHADES of bright yellow are a good choice for kitchens—they are uplifting for the people who gather there. Here, a cool acid yellow is combined with black to give a distinctly retro feel that is perfect for a sunny room. The naturally light environment allows such a starkly contrasting color combination to sing out and remain cheery.

PALE YELLOW is a calming, relaxing color. This means that, unlike the stronger, more energetic sunny or buttery yellows, it is a good choice for a person who wants a tranquil bedroom. It can create a bright and breezy atmosphere even in this small attic space. Note how this very light yellow manages to make the space appear to be larger than it really is, while a darker shade could have easily made the sloping ceiling appear somewhat claustrophobic. This particular yellow tint contains lots of white, so it is natural that pure white paint and fabrics—both on the ceiling and on the antique lace bedspread—look good combined with this shade. Meanwhile, the warm tones of the ornate brass bedstead emphasize the elements of underlying heat in this color scheme, making the room as a whole seem both fresh and vibrant.

From the palest primrose to exuberant buttercup, yellow is one of the most uplifting colors in the spectrum.

Sleek, well-designed lighting is central to contemporary room schemes.

BLACK ACCENTS seen against yellow painted walls have a particularly striking effect in this modernist living room. These two colors are often used in the world around us to denote the presence of danger, so this combination in a home interior creates a similar sense of drama. It is a bold and somewhat masculine scheme that is designed to be invigorating and stimulating rather than relaxing. Cushions, furnishing fabrics, lighting, and decorative accessories are all carefully coordinated to maintain the two-tone effect—even the dark metallic finish of the wood-burning stove is perfectly in keeping with the rest of the room.

EGG-YOLK YELLOW is an extremely lively color, which makes it a perfect choice when you want to make an area such as an entrance hall as welcoming as possible. It is a shade that works especially well in dark hallways that get little natural light of their own. The sunny brightness of such a glowing yellow easily compensates for the potential gloom of a room with small or nonexistent windows, while the naturally warm tones of wood further enhance the effect. The paintwork on the door and skirting boards has also been kept light. A generous armful of fresh flowers helps to create a lively and welcoming first impression.

Fresh flowers are always a welcoming sight, especially when chosen to coordinate with a room's decor.

good combinations

Blue and yellow are one of the happiest color marriages, evoking the balance to be found when you look at sea and sand, or sunflowers and summer skies. The nearer the blue moves toward purple—yellow's complementary—the more striking the results will be. So, use primary yellow and violet together in measured amounts with the sole purpose of creating a zingy impact, and you'll be able to make even this most unorthodox decorating combination work to your advantage. Alternatively, tone both colors down—using watery lemon beside pale lavender—and you'll find that these two colors can also form the basis of the softest color schemes.

Strong egg-yolk yellows are powerful colors, and so will need powerful companions. They look wonderful with ultramarine blue and fresh leafy green and are surprisingly appealing next to vibrant hot pinks, too. Try teaming them with pastels, for example, and the more subtle colors will seem insipid in comparison. Primrose and pale buttery yellows find much better companions in powder blues, mint greens, and dove grays.

Black and yellow are nature's warning colors, so if you're painting a room yellow, add dark-colored accents with care: the contrast could be harsh and startling.

Vibrant yellows are a good match for strong, deep blues —a combination that is both balanced and bouncy.

Yellow is contented beside blue, giving a fresh look reminiscent of sea and sand.

Next to gray, yellow takes on a cooler guise, while gray, in turn, will never look drab next to yellow.

A strong yolky yellow meets its match in a fresh, vibrant shade of grass green.

Golden yellow and hot pink form an unexpectedly rich and exotic combination.

Balancing primrose with a soft powder blue will bring a hint of spring to your surroundings.

Create instant sunshine by using warm, intense yellow amid an expanse of brilliant white.

warming accents

Yellow makes an excellent accent color to bring light and sunshine to a room. Use it to warm a cool color scheme of greens and blues or to add zest to a neutral scheme. It is no coincidence that Provençal interiors have deep yellows, bright lemons, and rich ochres as their hallmark; introduce any of these shades in order to recreate Mediterranean style.

green

GREEN is nature's hallmark, signifying life, freshness, and harmony. Adding it to your surroundings will be as uplifting as seeing the first leaves and shoots of spring. Though lime green is vibrant and energetic, in most of its guises green is wonderfully calm and relaxing, from palest sage and gentle celadon to stronger shades of bottle green and olive. This makes it one of the most versatile and easygoing color families to introduce into your home.

inspirations

If you're thinking of decorating a room in shades or tints of green, nature can offer a wealth of inspiration. You only have to glance at the brightness of a newly unfurled leaf, the subtlety of a shimmering willow, or the depth of green on a mossy stone and you'll be able to conjure up a wealth of colors that evoke the natural world.

Natural greens—from the brightest apple to the most subtle lichen—are a fantastic source of inspiration for the interior designer.

The highly descriptive names of the colors in this family reflect the limitless variety of options available to you as a designer. Think of the range of choices offered by anything from lime, mint, olive, and pistachio to apple, lichen, holly, and pea green, as well as bottle, hunting, and racing green, and you'll be able to pinpoint the precise shade that is most pleasing to your eye.

The vivid green of new grass is an uplifting shade because it represents life and fresh growth.

The natural sources from which green paints were originally derived were earth pigments and verdigris, an artificial pigment made from copper. Meanwhile, jade, emerald, malachite, and turquoise, which came originally from Egypt, are rarer and more expensive manifestations of green in the world around us.

Though bright greens were only widely used once the chrome yellow pigment had been discovered in the late 18th century, more muted, natural shades had been a familiar sight on the decorator's palette for centuries. The architect Robert Adam used gentle greens in his schemes; Victorian drawing rooms made the most of deep, somber shades; and William Morris used myriad greens as a symbol of the

Arts and Crafts Movement's return to natural forms and traditional values. This color family has proved equally popular on both sides of the Atlantic; dark muddy shades are instantly reminiscent of Shaker interiors, while Federal style shows cool, delicate gray-greens at their most attractive.

The moss-green shutters of a French cottage instantly conjure up rustic style.

These associations—both natural and historic— leave us with a sense that muted shades such as olive, sage, moss, and lichen are more at home in

A verdigris statue might inspire you to use pale, time-worn greens in your home.

relaxed, countrified settings such as kitchens and conservatories, while richer, darker greens such as bottle and forest dictate a more formal style. For this reason they traditionally adorn studies, dining rooms, and hall-ways. More recent trends for citrus shades have brought about the revival of zesty lime greens, which look good in a variety of contemporary settings. Pick and choose a shade according to the mood you'd like to create.

TERRA VERDE WASH FOR WALLS

*Using this very subtle green pigment you can create a hue
on your walls that is not easily identified as green,
but creates a beautiful, light yet warm atmosphere.*

INGREDIENTS

Coverage: approximately 48yds² (40m²)

- *1 gallon (5 liters) white paint*
- *brush or roller*
- *9¾oz (275g) green earth pigment*
- *4 quarts (4 liters) water*
- *glass jar*
- *¾ quart (0.75 liter) latex glazing liquid*
- *clean plastic bucket*
- *spoon*
- *small brush for edges*
- *large brush*
- *large sponge*

METHOD

■ For this color and finish it is important to have a good, solid white base coat, which has the absorbency to take a colorwash well, so paint your walls with white latex paint. If necessary apply two coats and leave to dry.

■ Soak the pigment in enough water to cover overnight, dissolving all the lumps. Prepare the latex glazing liquid in a bucket according to the instructions, using the rest of the water. Add the prepared pigment to the medium and stir well.

■ This wash is best applied in a cool, unheated room. Apply the colorwash using a small brush at the edges first, then covering the walls in a systematic pattern. Always finish one wall at a time. Leave to dry. Using the remainder of the color-wash, apply a second coat with a large sponge. Practice on some paper first.

SAFETY: always wear a dust mask when handling pigments

green   white latex paint

VICTORIAN-GREEN PAINT

*This green paint emulates one of the colors the Victorians
loved to have as a dramatic background for richly textured, patterned
fabrics and ornaments. It could work equally as well in a modern interior
and combines well with natural materials like linen, leather, wool,
and metal. Suitable for a study or living room.*

INGREDIENTS

Coverage: approximately 30yds² (25m²)

- *1 lb (500g) green pigment*
- *2–4¼ cups (0.5–1 liter) water*
- *glass jar*
- *2½ quarts (2.5 liters) white latex paint*
- *clean plastic bucket*
- *spoon*
- *small brush for edges*
- *large brush*

METHOD

■ Soak the pigment in enough water to
cover overnight, ensuring the mixture is
lump free. Add a little prepared pigment
to the latex paint in a bucket and stir
thoroughly. Continue adding pigment until
you obtain a color you are happy with
and paint a sample on the wall before
committing. Add some more water to
your mix if the paint becomes unwieldy.

■ Make sure the walls are smooth, clean,
and dust free and apply the paint
systematically, using a small brush at the
edges first. Work in an unheated, well-
ventilated room. You will need to apply
two coats, but always let the first coat dry
completely before applying a further one.

SAFETY: always wear a dust
mask when handling pigments

cerulean blue

oil glaze

turpentine

TURQUOISE-GREEN OIL GLAZE

*This glaze could be applied on top of the **Victorian-Green Paint** (see pp. 72–3) or to give an aged finish, or over any darker color from the green to blue range. Use on top of the **Ivory Distressed Finish** (see pp. 132–33) again for an antique look, or on top of light colors for a fresh aquatic look.*

INGREDIENTS

Coverage: up to 48yds^2 (40m^2)

- sandpaper
- ½–⅓oz (10–15g) cerulean blue pigment
- 1 quart (1 liter) turpentine or citrus peel oil thinner
- 2 cups (0.5 liter) transparent oil glaze
- spoon
- large glass jar with lid
- brush

METHOD

■ Sand smooth surfaces to provide a key. Mix the pigment with the thinner overnight, making sure that all lumps are well broken up. Stir the oil glaze and pour into a large, sealable glass jar. Add the prepared pigment and stir well.

■ In a well-ventilated room apply the glaze with a brush. Practice your brushing technique in an unobtrusive corner first if you wish. Always brush out the oil glaze well, to avoid drips.

SAFETY: always wear a dust mask when handling pigments and follow safety instructions when using oil-based products

green
black iron oxide
turpentine
floor and yacht varnish

DARK GREEN VARNISH

This is a lovely natural looking green that would look good on garden furniture or in a study or kitchen. This color will combine well with Plaster-colored Casein (see pp. 30–1).

INGREDIENTS

Coverage: approximately one chair.

- ⅚oz (24g) green pigment
- .03oz (1g) black iron oxide pigment
- 1 quart (1 liter) turpentine or oil thinner
- 2 clean glass jars
- 2 teaspoons
- 1 cup (0.25 liter) floor and yacht varnish
- large glass jar with lid
- spoon
- brush
- herb and resin oil (optional)

SAFETY: always wear a dust mask when handling pigments and follow safety instructions when working with oil-based products

METHOD

■ Soak the pigments separately in the thinner overnight. Grind the pigment into the thinner using the back of a teaspoon to create a smooth, lump-free paste. Transfer the varnish to a sealable glass jar and add the prepared green pigment. Stir thoroughly until a deep green color is consistent throughout. Slowly stir in some of the prepared black oxide pigment. This will darken the color so be sure to add it slowly and stop when you reach the desired depth of color. The color that you see in the jar will be very close to the dried result.

■ Make sure your wood is clean and dry before application. Prime very dry or absorbent wood with herb and resin oil. Apply your dark green varnish systematically, working it into the wood where necessary. Apply at least two coats for floors or exterior use, allowing each coat to dry thoroughly before applying the next one.

healing with green

GREEN IN FENG SHUI

As its position at the center of the color spectrum indicates, green has a balancing energy and an inherent sense of harmony. The practice of feng shui links it to the wood element, so—like trees themselves—green has come to symbolize health, growth, and vitality. You can enhance these life-giving properties by painting an interior green, introducing foliage plants, or using lots of natural materials such as wicker, bamboo, and bare wood. Choose green for bedrooms or living rooms, or anywhere you'd like to be nourished and nurtured.

BELOW *Green rooms, dominated by natural materials and plants, are harmonious spaces, ideal for family living.*

A living room painted green brings all the color's positive associations—health, life, and well-being—to the heart of family life.

Verdant foliage plants are vauluable in the practice of feng shui because they resto vitality to dark corners.

Natural materials such as wood and wicker wil enhance green's life-givir properties.

Green also encourages good fortune to enter our lives. Although this can include material wealth, it also encompasses our children, family, and friends.

GREEN IN COLOR THERAPY

The fact that green surrounds us in nature contributes to its traditional associations as the color of healing and relaxation. It appears to play an important role in restoring mental equilibrium, but is also linked with some rather more fundamental aspects of the body's function—the heart, lungs, thymus, and circulatory system. For this reason, color therapists use it to alleviate a variety of problems ranging from nervous disorders to high blood pressure. Green also has an important role to play in restoring a spiritual perspective to our lives, connecting body and soul and bringing about a deep sense of peace and tranquility. Consider green—either on expanses of walls or as accents via plants or a variety of accessories—for rooms where you tend to relax and reflect on your life.

GREEN AND YOUR HEALTH

Green can alleviate:

- stress
- hypertension
- asthma and bronchitis
- poor circulation
- allergies

Green can aggravate:

- lethargy
- jealousy
- autoimmune problems
- resentment
- nausea

real life

Nature's paint box is alive with shades of green, from the bright spring green of new shoots, the mid-green of summer grass, to subtle mossy tints and forest greens. Use green in your home for a restful atmosphere, or create a more energizing effect by juxtaposing contrasting shades.

Fresh flowers can be used to introduce a splash of contrasting color to a room. Here, yellow acts as a warming influence on the cool shades that are seen on walls and soft furnishings.

THE STRESS-RELIEVING and emotionally balancing qualities of green make it a great choice for bedrooms. This charming attic room has a rough plaster finish and numerous angles: using pale jade all over helps to unify its appearance. Green is a naturally healing and nurturing color. Here, these properties are intensified by the presence of bare wood, simple fabrics, and garden flowers. No other decoration is necessary—the room's uncomplicated coziness proves that less can be more.

THE ENTRANCE HALL is a busy place in any house, yet here the choice of color—a soft, serene, pale sage—calms the scene of activity beautifully. Combined with a rich farmhouse cream on the walls, this particular shade of green is tranquil and rustic, making it very well-suited to its country setting. It injects vitality without being overpowering and is bright enough to maintain valuable light levels despite the confined space. Green is also a traditionally welcoming color, so this scheme makes an ideal first impression on anyone entering the house. If you decide on green, choose your shade carefully, according to whether you prefer to feel cool and relaxed (mint or sea green), bright and optimistic (apple or lime), or to be hidden deep in a forest glade (bottle or olive).

To enhance a room scheme, line a sunny windowsill with a row of bottle-green glassware and, as the light shines through, revel in their glowing colors.

To give a room a sense of coherence, bring together its dominant colors in a two-tone floor. Linoleum or ceramic tiles work well; alternatively, paint a checkerboard design directly onto the floorboards.

Remember that accessories and cosmetics displayed artfully can play an important part in your bathroom's color scheme.

A NATURALLY UPLIFTING shade of pale sea green is a refreshing choice for a bathroom, where it offers a successful alternative to the more traditional blue. It is especially cool and clean when combined with classic white fittings and a checkerboard tiled floor.

Mint greens can seem cold if natural light levels are low, so save them for the sunniest parts of the house. Alternatively, to provide a burst of heat, try lining shelves and window-sills with a row of terra-cotta pots.

 GREENS THAT ARE MIXED with a dominant amount of yellow to produce a pale, light shade are warm and stimulating. This effect is strengthened when accents of contrasting colors, such as pinks and reds, are scattered around. That is why this simple, spacious bedroom seems so vibrant, homey, and comfortable. Traditional red gingham cushions, a floral bedspread with pink accents, and a pretty woven pink and white runner introduce these warmer shades, while plenty of white paint on the floorboards, fireplace, and wardrobe lightens the effect of the antique-style dark wood desk and armchair.

Jaunty ginghams are a good foil for greens, recreating a folk-art feel.

good combinations

Imagine the way the colors of a verdant summer landscape blend together effortlessly, and see how adding plants gives any room an instant lift, and you will understand that green looks good in any setting. In particular, green works wonderfully with reds of a similar tone: try deep bottle green with touches of crimson, terra-cotta with olive, or sage with plaster pink. Harmonious rooms can also be designed by combining green with blue or yellow. For pleasing green and blue schemes try dark forest green with deep navy; olive with French navy; lime with turquoise; or apple with sky blue. For green and yellow schemes, consider fresh beech-leaf green with egg yolk; moss with gold; mint with butter; or pistachio with primrose.

The fact that the green color family has deep roots in the natural world means that all its shades combine effortlessly with all manner of neutrals, from stone and mushroom to cream and dove-gray, the paler shades lifting and offsetting the greens to perfection. It is easy to find well-matched pairs that are wonderfully restful, like lichen and stone, pistachio and cream, and holly and buff, for example.

Green and white make a lively combination that always appears fresh, clean, and unfussy.

Add a splash of red—green's complementary—to make the colors really sing out.

Citrus shades come together in this fresh combination of orange and lime.

For a wonderfully subtle scheme, combine sage green with delicate plaster pink.

Green and purple form a regal color palette that works best in the presence of white.

For a vibrant, eye-opening scheme, try pairing fresh bright greens with strong pinks.

Neighbors on the color wheel, green and yellow make well-matched decorating partners.

neutral combinations

Green is often described as a neutral color—in other words, it is neither overwhelmingly hot or cold, nor advancing or receding. Greens can take on different characteristics depending on the amount of blue or yellow they contain. As a rule, green may be combined with a surprising number of different hues.

blue

BLUE is a magical color—uplifting, relaxing, serene, and inspiring all at once. It might be cool, but it doesn't have to be cold: the tranquility of pale blue, reminiscent of endless summer skies, brings with it a sense of infinite space and peace; the electric vitality of aquamarine and cobalt are stimulating and refreshing; the deep shades of navy and denim are timeless classics.

inspirations

When deciding on the best shade for your scheme, a garden of blue flowers will provide a patchwork of hues to inspire you. You may be drawn to a swath of cornflowers, a cluster of campanulas, a bluebell wood, a carpet of forget-me-nots, the first grape hyacinths of spring, some elegant irises, a delicate wisteria, tall spires of delphiniums or a windowbox brimming with vivacious pansies. Match your color schemes to the richness of these blooms and you'll bring the tranquility of the natural world into your home.

Transport yourself to warmer climes by using the intense blues of sky and sea combined with the bright shades characteristic of Greek fishing villages and Caribbean islands or the azure seen all over the Mediterranean. Such blues, which have a rich base and a natural warmth, will recreate the heat and intensity of these countries wherever you live. Everyday items around the house might also spark off a blue-based color scheme: try fabrics such as ginghams, tickings, and toiles, glass such as pharmacy bottles and Bristolware, or ceramics such as willow-pattern china, Delft tiles, Wedgwood jasperware, or striped Cornish pottery. All provide classic variations on the blue theme. Natural earth pigments gave the early decorators a wide range of reds, browns,

Mussel shells display a beautifully subtle range of pale blues, purples, and deep inky blues.

Look to the garden to find your favorite shade of blue. Match your paint color to the first grape hyacinths of spring and your interior will seem calm and uplifting.

ochres, grays, and greens, but not blues, which meant that this color was a latecomer to home interiors. Bright, warm shades of blue could be obtained at a price from the exotic and expensive mineral lapis lazuli. This was so costly, however, that its use was mainly restricted to the world of fine art, where it was used, for example, to depict the glowing tones of the Madonna's robes. Instead, the earliest blues to appear in any quantity in Europe were obtained from indigo, an organic vegetable dye imported from Asia. It produced blues that were cool, deep, and soft shades that were strong but never as luminous as lapis.

Washed-out denim provides a subtle palette of dusty blues that could well inspire a room scheme. Use the fabric itself to cover soft furnishings— chair covers and cushions will age just as gracefully as your favorite pair of jeans.

Prussian blue—a cool, dark, inky shade—was seen on decorators' palettes by the middle of the 18th century, yet still bright, rich, warm blues remained out of reach for most people. That was until the 19th century, when cobalt blue was introduced and when ultramarine blue began to be manufactured synthetically. These wonderfully intense hues then started to appear in interiors to intoxicating effect—they were a favorite of Robert Adam, for example, whose designs show them used along with bright greens and pure reds. After that, decorators never looked back and now, the variety of blues to choose from is enormous.

Bright blues are instantly reminiscent of the Greek islands, where this vibrant sun-enhanced shade is a traditional favorite.

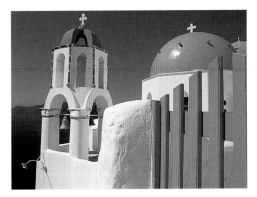

ultra marine blue

casein milk paint

POWDER-BLUE CASEIN

This is a beautiful, cool color and finish, proven to suit many different styles of interiors, including kitchens, hallways, and bathrooms. For kitchens and particularly bathrooms you might want to harden the finish by applying one or two coats of generously thinned clear latex glazing liquid on top of the finish.

INGREDIENTS

Coverage: approximately 48yds² (40m²)

- 5¼oz (150g) ultramarine blue pigment
- 1⅓ gallon (5 liters) water
- glass jar
- 9lbs (4kg) casein milk paint (distemper)
- clean plastic bucket
- spoon
- small brush for edges
- large brush

METHOD

■ Soak the pigment in enough water to cover overnight. Prepare the casein milk paint in a bucket according to the instructions, using the rest of the water. Prime an absorbent surface with a coat of milk paint. Add the prepared pigment to the paint and stir until the paint has the consistency of whipping cream.

■ In a cool, ventilated room, paint the edges of the room first using the small brush, then use the large brush and apply the paint systematically working from top to bottom, finishing one wall at a time. The translucent milk paint becomes opaque when dry. Allow one coat to dry completely before applying another. Casein milkpaint should dry to a completely flat finish and is quite hard-wearing if applied properly.

SAFETY: always wear a dust mask when handling pigments

VIBRANT BLUE OIL GLAZE

Especially effective in bathrooms and kitchens, this glaze will work on most surfaces including wood, paper, and plastics. The glaze works well over pastel-colored surfaces, but remember that the color and texture of the wall beneath will show through.

INGREDIENTS

Coverage: approximately 24yds² (20m²)

- sandpaper
- 1¾oz (50g) ultramarine blue pigment
- 1 tsp ultramarine violet pigment
- 1 tsp zinc white pigment
- 2 cups (0.5 liter) turpentine or citrus peel oil thinner
- glass jar
- teaspoon
- 1½ quarts (1.5 liters) transparent oil glaze
- large glass jar with lid
- spoon
- brush

METHOD

■ Sand smooth surfaces to provide a good key. Mix all the dry pigments together and soak them in enough thinner to cover overnight. Use the back of a teaspoon to break up any lumps and create a smooth paste. Stir the oil glaze well and pour into a large sealable glass jar. Add the prepared pigments and stir well, then stir in the remaining thinner.

■ Working in a well-ventilated room, apply the oil glaze with a brush. Always brush the glaze out well so you don't get drips and runs.

SAFETY: always wear a dust mask when handling pigments and follow safety instructions when working with oil-based products

cerulean blue · ultramarine blue · beeswax

TURQUOISE-BLUE LIMING WAX

This decorative finish for interior wood looks great in a kitchen, living room, or bathroom. It is similar in effect to traditional liming wax, but adopts a simpler method of application and uses an unusual color combination.

INGREDIENTS

Coverage: approximately one dresser or four chairs

- ¾oz (20g) cerulean blue pigment
- ⅓oz (10g) ultramarine blue pigment
- 2 teaspoons
- saucer
- 3½oz (100g) beeswax-based furniture wax
- cotton rags for applying
- cotton rag or shoe brush for polishing
- polishing brush (optional)

SAFETY: always wear a dust mask when handling pigments and follow safety instructions when working with wax products

METHOD

- Use previously untreated wood, stripped pine, or even a cheap plywood with a blond, porous surface.
- Sprinkle one teaspoon of ultramarine blue pigment and two teaspoons of cerulean blue pigment on a saucer and combine. Use a rag to pick up some wax and dip it gently into your pigment mix.
- In a well-ventilated room, practice applying the wax and pigment on a sample board first to establish how much pigment you would like to apply. Using pressure to force the wax and pigment into all the pores and cracks in the wood will color and fill them. Continue rubbing the wood with wax until the whole surface is covered. Use a clean rag or polishing brush to buff the wax to a lovely sheen and lasting finish.

white latex paint · ultramarine blue

BRUSHED PAINT WASHES

These washes are easy and fun to work with. They look lovely in any room and suit many modern schemes.

INGREDIENTS

Coverage: approximately 48yds² (40m²)

- ½ gallon (1.5 liters) white latex paint
- 3 plastic containers with lids
- 2½oz (75g) ultramarine blue pigment
- 2¼ gallons (8.5 liters) water
- glass jar
- 3 spoons
- small brush for edges
- large brush
- clean brush to remove brush marks

SAFETY: always wear a dust mask when handling pigments

METHOD

■ Divide the paint into three equal parts in three sealable plastic containers. Soak the pigment overnight in enough water to cover, dispersing any lumps. To make three paint washes with varying degrees of intensity, add different quantities of pigment to each paint. Mix up each paint wash only when you are ready to use it. This keeps the paint fresh and lets you adjust your coloring in accordance with the dried result of the previous layer. To the first paint add 2 tsps of pigment and ¼–½ gallon (1–2.5 liters) of water (the amount of water won't change the color but will alter the opaqueness of the finish). To the second add 4 tsps of pigment and water. To the third add 6 tsps of pigment and water.

■ Apply the lightest wash first, using a small brush at the edges and brushing out in all directions. Always keep your paint wash well-stirred. Lightly brush over the surface with a clean brush to remove brush marks. Leave to dry completely before applying the next coat.

healing with blue

BLUE IN FENG SHUI

Blue has a natural affinity with water and so shares with this element the potential to be either wonderfully still and calming or freely flowing and liberated. To followers of feng shui, blue therefore represents both your inner tranquility and your path in life. If your existence seems stagnant or directionless, then introducing blue to your home, along with water—perhaps an indoor fountain—or glass—blue bottles would be ideal—and these may well help it flow toward fulfillment once again.

BELOW Blue promotes inner calm and helps foster understanding—for this reason, you may choose to decorate your study or workroom in this palette.

A study with blue walls represents the quest for power and knowledge. It may even advance your career.

A desk surrounded by blue clears the mind and promotes lucid thinking.

Red will balance blue's tendency to appear cold and will add an invigorating burst of energy.

The presence of blue in your surroundings also represents your potential for learning and understanding, since the depth of the ocean symbolizes the vast reserves of knowledge and creativity that await you. Painting your study blue would therefore stimulate learning, encourage new thought processes, and even improve your career prospects.

BLUE IN COLOR THERAPY

Blue governs the throat and the thyroid, so has an important role to play both in speech and communication and in the body's metabolic functions. It also engenders a sense of calm and relaxation, which is why it promotes healing, relieves pain and restores health. Blue is therefore a naturally good color to choose if you're decorating a bedroom since it can help you sleep more deeply and more peacefully. It is also recommended in therapy rooms, where it will aid recovery, and in offices and workrooms, where it will enhance learning and self-cultivation as well as promote clear thinking.

BLUE AND YOUR HEALTH

Blue can alleviate:	Blue can aggravate:
■ insomnia	■ melancholia
■ nerves	■ chilliness
■ shock	■ isolation
■ anxiety	■ seasonal affective
■ lack of	disorder
self-confidence	■ garrulousness

real life

Don't ignore blue because you think it will add a harsh coldness to a room—there are shades that are meditative, give an impression of spaciousness, impart vitality, or add a touch of class.

VERY EFFECTIVE FOR WATERY schemes in bathrooms, blues combine well to create effortless beach-house style. Here, turquoise-painted tongue-and-groove boarding sits happily beside the royal blue of the bathtub and the French navy of the stained floorboards. If there's any doubt as to the seaside setting, pebbles gathered from the beach nestle beneath the tub. This is a good example of how color can transform the simplest of settings—there's nothing particularly sophisticated about the basic elements that are combined in this room, yet with a wash of harmonious paint colors the result is wonderfully atmospheric.

Gather blue-gray pebbles from the beach and display them in your bathroom to complement its seaside theme.

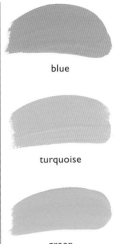

blue

turquoise

green

THE COLOR TURQUOISE is something of a chameleon; people perceive it as blue beside blue and as green beside green. Using turquoise as the main background color in this drawing room, and then combining it with a variety of accent shades of blue and green, creates a visually complex scheme that plays many a trick on the eye. You are never quite sure whether blue or green predominates, but the overall effect is certainly harmonious. To remind yourself why, look back at the color wheel and you'll see that all these shades sit close together in the spectrum.

Mosaic tiles bring together a host of watery shades including turquoise and royal blue. Use them to enhance the decor of bathrooms.

A SHADY CORNER of a garden terrace takes on a distinctly Mediterranean style thanks to an inspired use of color. A shade of blue that instantly transports you to the Greek Ionian Sea has been used on the window frame and on the rustic wooden table, where it is combined with a warm sea-green. These colors are then picked up again in cushions arranged on a relaxing daybed and on a variety of plant pots clustered together on a garden table. A dish of pebbles sits on the main table to underline the seaside theme and bring the beach even closer to home.

Blue and white make a classic mix that always seems fresh. Combine accessories and paints with fabrics such as gingham to create a timeless sense of style.

BLUE ROOMS don't have to be cold—this electric Matisse blue creates a cozy family kitchen that positively glows with warmth and vibrant color. Though the tubular steel shelving and sleek work-tops give it a thoroughly modern slant, the overall scheme also has some very traditional elements; striped Cornishware storage jars on the counter top and a gingham curtain gathered beneath the sink are old-fashioned blue-and-white favorites that have filled kitchens for centuries. Blue is a good choice in rooms that are usually filled with activity since it promotes cool, calm, and collected thought despite the other distractions.

Comb antiques shops, junk shops, and flea markets for old glass medicine bottles, whose vivid colors enhance any blue room scheme.

good combinations

Blue and white are perhaps one of the most time-honored color combinations—blissfully simple and practically foolproof, yet unfailingly fresh, crisp, and uplifting. Whether you use blocks of sky blue to recreate marine style in a seaside cottage or introduce navy for a more sophisticated look, white is almost always the perfect partner.

Many people shy away from using expanses of blue in interiors because it is considered aloof and unwelcoming. This is not always the case, but, to make sure your scheme is not icy, combine it with touches of orange—blue's complementary color—somewhere in the room. Along with yellows, reds, and terra-cottas, these combinations will bring instant heat to blue schemes, but think carefully before combining green with a cool blue.

A modern take on traditional blue-and-white china, this subtle yet simple crockery would complement a kitchen decorated in cool blues.

Blue is surprisingly easygoing when seen next to a range of other colors; there really are very few partnerships that are out of bounds, providing the tonal relationships remain balanced. Experiment by teaming duck-egg blue with cream, royal blue with emerald, baby blue with primrose, denim with salmon pink, ultramarine blue with gold, or navy blue with burnt orange.

Blue and white are old favorites that are at their best when combined in sunny locations.

For a room that gets little natural light, cream makes a warmer companion for pale blue.

Strong blue used with emerald green makes for a balanced and harmonious combination.

Make an eye-catching scene by using blue with orange, its complementary color.

You can add heat to a blue room by adding an expanse of golden yellow.

Pink and blue will take on a more contemporary style if you select strong shades of each.

heating up blue

Some shades of blue appear icier than others and it is generally held that mixing lots of different shades of blue in the same room does intensify the color's chilliness. To create warmer blue schemes, you can choose a range of naturally warm shades such as Matisse blue, royal blue, turquoise, vivid ultramarine blue, or pinky lilac.

2

purple

FROM deep, regal purple to the softest, gentlest
mauves, this color family is rich in decorating
possibilities. Violet has the shortest wavelength and
the fastest vibration in the color spectrum, so its
light is cleansing and calming—interiors filled with
sweet lilac or dusty plum have a powerful effect on
our emotions, while the soft tones of lavender are
as soothing as the herb itself.

inspirations

Dark purple inspires images of pomp and ceremony thanks to it being the color of choice for the robes of Roman emperors and royalty over the ages. These precious and majestic qualities meant it was rarely used outside such exclusive circles until the rococo period, when an elegant shade of pale lilac became one of the pastel colors favored by the French king's mistress Madame de Pompadour.

Brownish purples seen in the kitchen garden may prompt you to create rich yet subtle decorative schemes.

Bright, rich purples surfaced again when classical styles were revived in the late 18th century. Then, when new dyes were introduced in the decades that followed, the choice was even greater, and modish shades of deep mauve appeared as a favorite among grand Victorian householders.

Nowadays, it is the paler forms of the color that appear to be the most popular among decorators. The more intense and dominating purples tend to be reserved for use as restrained splashes of color —perhaps on fabrics or as eye-catching accessories

In late summer the lavender fields of Provence are a mass of palest purples and soft dusty greens—a sight to inspire a decorating scheme.

—because they can seem over-powering on a large scale.

A visit to Provence, in France, in the late summer is enough to make anyone fall in love with these palest shades of purple. The color and scent of the lavender fields produces a heady and sensual mix that can be recreated

in interiors with the subtlest shade of latex paint on the walls and a few drops of essential oil vaporizing in a burner.

There's plenty of inspiration to be found closer to home, especially in the garden: imagine lilac trees laden with blooms, delicate violets nestling in the shade, a trellis entwined with the richly hued flowers of a clematis or the papery petals of some sweet peas, the tall fronds of a hollyhock, exuberant hydrangeas, a collection of pansies, or a pot of purple-leafed sage. All can form a basis for the prettiest, most summery schemes.

Transfer the deep, dusty shades of ripening grapes to your decorating palette.

Meanwhile, in the kitchen, the glossy skin of an eggplant, a dewy cluster of red grapes, the subtle shades of some beets, a red onion or cabbage, or a bowl of freshly harvested plums might spark off

Andre Chrysenaar's Woman in Lilac illustrates the soothing qualities of this color.

similar ideas for decorating with accents of deep purple.

In the garden and hedges you can see the berry shades that are particularly attractive for room schemes with an autumnal air—shades of crushed blackberry, blueberry, and raspberry are deliciously evocative of the mellow harvest season. While these colors might be too deep for the walls themselves, they translate particularly well to soft furnishings, where the rich textures of velvets, linens, and damasks complement their deep hues.

LIGHT AND ELEGANT LATEX PAINT

*This is a subtle and cool color that would go
well with both traditional and ultra-modern interiors.
Suitable for halls, dining rooms, and bedrooms.*

INGREDIENTS

Coverage: approximately 24yds² (20m²)

- *3½oz (100g) Mars violet pigment
  (caput mortuum)*
- *1 quart (1 liter) water*
- *glass jar*
- *½ gallon (1.5 liters) white latex paint*
- *clean plastic bucket*
- *spoon*
- *small brush for edges*
- *large brush*

METHOD

■ Soak the pigment in a jar with enough
water to cover overnight, making sure any
lumps are dissolved. Add the prepared
pigment to the white latex paint in a
plastic bucket and mix thoroughly.

■ Before application make sure your
wall surface is sound and clean. In a
ventilated room, paint systematically,
using a small brush at the edges first
and finishing one wall at a time. You will
need to apply two coats, but always let
the first coat dry completely before
applying the next.

SAFETY: always wear a dust
mask when handling pigments

DRAGGING ON PAINTED WOOD

*Dragging is a traditional finishing effect often carried out over painted wood. In order to be successful a smooth and even surface should be chosen and you need a steady hand to make a regular pattern. Purple is a strong color which, when used in a broken-color effect like this one, appears much softer. Try this finish on top of the **Gray Wood Stain** (see pp. 134–5) or an existing light paint finish like a white eggshell.*

INGREDIENTS

Coverage: approximately 12yds² (10m²)

- 1oz (30g) ultramarine violet pigment
- ⅓ cup (.1 liter) turpentine or thinner
- glass jar
- teaspoon
- ½ quart (0.5 liter) linseed oil varnish
- large glass jar with lid
- spoon
- brush
- dragging brush

METHOD

■ Soak the pigment in the turpentine overnight. Use the back of a teaspoon to break up any lumps and create a smooth paste. Pour the varnish into a sealable container and add the prepared pigment. Stir thoroughly.

■ In a well-ventilated room, use a brush to apply the mixture over a surface that has already been painted white or a light shade. Use the dragging brush to draw long uninterrupted lines through the still-wet varnish, from top to bottom or from side to side across the surface. Continue making parallel lines until the whole surface has been dragged. Work quickly and evenly. Allow to dry overnight.

SAFETY: always wear a dust mask when handling pigments and follow safety instructions when working with oil-based products

ULTRAMARINE VIOLET CASEIN

*This is a striking color with a traditional looking finish. It would look good on a single wall in an overall lighter purple scheme, for example in combination with the **Light and Elegant Latex Paint** (see pp. 110–11).*

INGREDIENTS

Coverage: approximately 24yds^2 (20m^2)

- *14oz (400g) ultramarine violet pigment*
- *2 quarts (2 liters) water*
- *glass jar*
- *4½lbs (2kg) casein milk paint (distemper)*
- *clean plastic bucket*
- *spoon*
- *small brush for edges*
- *large brush for covering*

METHOD

- Soak the pigment in enough water to cover overnight, ensuring any lumps are dissolved. Prepare the casein milk paint in a bucket according to the instructions, using the rest of the water. Prime absorbent surfaces with uncolored milk paint. Add the prepared pigment to the paint and stir thoroughly until it has the consistency of whipping cream.

- In a cool, ventilated room, paint the edges of the room first using a small brush, then use a large brush to apply the milk paint systematically, working from top to bottom and always finishing one wall at a time. The translucent milk paint becomes opaque when dry. Allow one coat to dry completely before applying another. Milk paint should dry to a smooth, flat finish and is hard-wearing if properly applied.

SAFETY: always wear a dust mask when handling pigments

PURPLE WOOD STAIN

This is a strong and moody stain for all light-colored woods. Suitable for a teenager's room, a 1960s inspired hall or stairwell, and the kitchen. Also good for woodwork, furniture, and built-in units.

INGREDIENTS

Coverage: approximately 9½yds² (8m²)

- ⅔oz (20g) ultramarine violet pigment
- ⅔oz (20g) Mars violet pigment (crocus martis)
- 1 cup (0.25 liter) turpentine or thinner
- 2 glass jars
- 2 teaspoons
- 2 cups (0.5 liter) linseed oil varnish
- large glass jar with lid
- spoon
- brush

METHOD

■ Soak each of the pigments individually in half the thinner overnight. Grind the mixtures with the back of the teaspoons to create a smooth paste. Transfer the varnish to a sealable glass jar and add both of the prepared pigments. Stir thoroughly.

■ Do not prime wood but before application make sure it is clean and dry. In a well-ventilated room, apply the stain with a brush, working it into the wood. Apply one coat only for interior use and two or three coats for exterior use. Dilute the stain with more thinner if the color is too strong.

SAFETY: always wear a dust mask when handling pigments and follow safety instructions when working with oil-based products

healing
with purple

PURPLE IN FENG SHUI

The feng shui of purple depends largely on whether the shade you choose is dominated by blue or red. Bluish purples share much in common with blue itself; they are linked to the water element and bring with them the power to calm and to generate self-discovery. Reddish violets are potent because they are fiery—they tend to bring passion to the rooms in which they are used.

Meanwhile, lavender and mauve—perhaps the most common decorating colors from the

BELOW *Creativity can be enhanced by working in a room painted in shades of pale purple. Darker versions of this color can inspire passion and self-discovery.*

Purple surroundings will encourage you to explore your spirituality.

For men and women alike, purple workrooms will increase creativity.

Bluish purples are the most calming and relaxing shades in this color family.

Reddish purples and violets are the most stimulating.

purple family—are too pale to stimulate a room's energy significantly. Instead it is considered that they enhance the spirituality of their surroundings—ideal if you want to create a quiet space in which to carry out creative tasks or meditation.

PURPLE IN COLOR THERAPY

Violet is a powerful tool in terms of color therapy. It is the color associated with the crown of the head, so—on a purely physiological level—it has a powerful effect on the brain and central nervous system. But it also operates on a spiritual plane since it is linked to the higher self and the psyche. In this sense, this color can be used to promote religious health, artistic endeavor, deep inspiration, and mental balance. Shades of purple—and purple crystals such as amethyst—are therefore thought to be particularly therapeutic in rooms where you intend to devote time to being quiet and introspective—bedrooms, studies, and therapy rooms, for example, would all benefit from this color's ability to bring about profound changes in our lives.

PURPLE AND YOUR HEALTH

Purple can alleviate:
- lack of creativity
- slow-wittedness
- depression
- lack of motivation
- lack of spiritual direction

Purple can aggravate:
- serious emotional problems
- addictive personalities
- shyness
- antisocial behavior
- alienation

real life

Purple has many associations—dusky berry tones are reminiscent of autumn, violet is mystical, rich purple is a badge of royalty and status, delicate lilac and lavender have the fresh appeal of fragrant flowers. It's not as difficult to use as you might think, and you can even inject highlights of yellow or pink to add zing to your color scheme.

Remember that white dilutes intense purples and prevents them from becoming muddy or saccharine.

PALE PURPLE is both cleansing and calming, which is why this bedroom, inspired by the softness of lilac and lavender, seems so inviting. Using lots of white beside these soft bluish purples keeps them bright and fresh, especially when the room is drenched in plenty of sunlight. Color therapists use such shades of pale purple to promote relaxation and clear thinking as well as to improve physical health, particularly where tension, nervous disorders, and depression are indicated.

THIS MINIMALLY decorated hallway is a lovely example of an interior that revels in color for its own sake; no other adornment is required here apart from a rich and regal shade of purple covering one wall—it's all the room needs to bring it alive and excite the eye. This scheme makes the most of a distinctly bluish shade of purple, which is cooler and more tranquil than a redder shade would have been in the same setting (warmer purples look hotter and more vibrant than their bluer cousins and are more stimulating both to the emotions and the senses). Nevertheless, lots of white is still needed next to such a bold, deep color in order to keep the light levels high and balance the color's richness and intensity.

You can add shades of purple to a room through accessories such as throws and rugs. The more interesting their textures, the richer the overall effect.

A DUSTY MAUVE COLORWASH provides a pleasant finish against which to view a collection of plaster busts and ceramics. This paint effect builds up layers of dilute pigment to create an intentionally uneven surface reminiscent of aged or sun-bleached walls. The shade used here is one of the most easy-going purples you can choose—it's neither so dark that it's gloomy nor so pale that it's insipid. Yet it brings with it all the potency and impact of this highly sophisticated color family.

Purples containing red appear warm; those dominated by blue are cool.

In boldly decorated rooms, accessories in similarly vivid shades are the perfect finishing touch.

EVEN IN ITS VARIOUS TINTS and shades, purple gives its surroundings a sense of grandeur, a quality that is intensified in this sophisticated living room by the inclusion of rich fabrics and marble paneling. One of the best partners for purple is green, the color with which it blends so effortlessly in nature. Following the basic tenet about combining colors that are of a similar tone in order to keep the room in balance, we know that plum sits easily beside forest green, while lavender looks happiest with sage. In this elegant drawing room, a gentle mauve and mint partnership follows this rule to the letter.

good combinations

One of the happiest companions for purple is green. In nature, it is the color's perfect foil—witness the clever balance between the soft green foliage of a lavender bush and its delicate flowering spires, or the happy marriage between the deep green leaves of a rhododendron and its bright purple blooms. Use these to inspire combinations such as lilac and sage or eggplant and olive, remembering to match tones to ensure the room stays in balance.

Another useful ingredient in purple color schemes is white, which counterbalances the intensity of purple. White is especially valuable in rooms which have low levels of natural light, which can sometimes make darker purples look morbid. Also, use white with gentler shades of mauve and you'll prevent a saccharine appearance; use it with lilac and you'll keep the look clean and fresh.

Green and purple often sit happily next to one another in the natural world, so let the pairings you see in woods and fields dictate the shades you put together in your home.

Yellow is enlivening when used along with purple, because it is its complementary. This can be seen in the starkest contrast by placing pure violet next to primary yellow and is a useful color combination to remember when you want to "lift" a purple scheme and prevent it from seeming too somber.

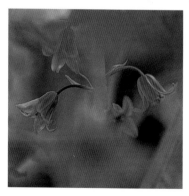

124

If you take a leaf out of nature's book, green and purple combine with great ease.

Rich purple paint can be balanced and brightened by using plenty of plain white paint.

Lilac and pale blue are well-matched tonally, which makes them a truly relaxing partnership.

The zingy juxtaposition of complementaries purple and yellow is particularly striking.

A primrose-yellow wall sits happily with a soft purple sofa in this gentle combination.

Violet and lilac is an unusual combination but can be made to work if the tones are well-matched.

purples and pastels

Soft purples are always attractive next to other pastels; with powder blue on its own they may seem cold, but add a touch of rose pink or creamy yellow and the whole scheme will seem bright and sunny.

black and
white

ALTHOUGH not strictly colors because they are not part of the color wheel, black, white, and the grays formed from them are indispensable to the interior designer. Touches of pure black—an absence of any color or light—can be used to accent or set off other colors in a room. In stark contrast is white—the result of combining all the colors in the spectrum in perfect balance—which is a mainstay of many home interiors, the basis of pure, clean, cool, bright, and simple schemes.

inspirations

Black is a difficult color to use in interiors because it can bring with it a range of negative associations— its links with evil, depression, and mourning are inescapable. Yet used judiciously it can also be highly sophisticated; all-black walls and ceilings were considered to be the height of fashion in the 1920s, for example. Now, however, black is more commonly reserved for use as an accent color—that is, a visual trick played by interior designers to focus the eye on certain details or make adjacent colors sing out in contrast.

Mixing black and white gives an array of delicate grays, ranging from stone and dove to the watery color of a winter's sky.

The deepest, densest blacks are reminiscent of jet, obsidian, and ebony, but bear in mind that these can be the least forgiving when used *en masse*. Instead, you might consider using closely related tones such as charcoal (deep gray), slate (dark blue-gray), and ink (intense blue-black)—these are particularly striking when covering smaller areas such as woodwork or flooring and can be incorpo-

Seen together, black and white make a wonderfully strong impression. In the home, reserve this partnership for striking modernist schemes, or use black sparingly to draw the eye to a particular detail.

rated into your home in a way that is gentle on the eye as well as on the emotions.

The widespread use of both chalk- and lime-based white paints since time immemorial makes them something of a staple —think of the traditional white-washes on both the interior and exterior of a multitude of country cottages and you'll realize the extent to which we have always considered white to be a safe and acceptable—although not unexciting—color to use for our surroundings.

When considering decorating with white let yourself be inspired by nature's examples: think of a snowy landscape, the subtlety of marble, the plumage of a swan, the finest porcelain clay, or a vase of elegant lilies.

The brilliant whites that are widely used today are a relatively recent phenomenon. Their distinctly bluish and sometimes harsh tinge actually results from the inclusion of titanium oxide, a mineral pigment that only became available in the 1920s. Before that, white was a somewhat more unstable color that began to turn yellow over time.

Many people still love the mellowness of these traditional whites, which has led to a recent revival of old favorites such as milk paints and whitewashes. These are valuable to the decorator because they often contain a hint of another color, making them gentler and more versatile than brilliant white, especially in rooms lit by harsh artificial light. Modern paint ranges now emulate this by featuring colors such as warm whites (which include a touch of yellow, red, or brown) or cool whites (which will include a touch of gray, black, or blue).

A Grecian marble statue epitomizes the elegance of rich, creamy off-whites.

Contrasts in black and white are demonstrated again in this 18th-century Chinese lacquer box.

black iron oxide

umber

turpentine

linseed oil vanish

EBONY WOOD STAIN

*This stain is suitable on all absorbent wood,
and looks great on floors and furniture.*

INGREDIENTS

Coverage: approximately 9½yds² (8m²)

- 1¼oz (35g) black iron oxide pigment
- ¼oz (5g) umber pigment
- ⅓ cup (0.1 liter) turpentine or thinner
- glass jar
- teaspoon
- ½ quart (.5 liter) linseed oil varnish
- large glass jar with lid
- spoon
- brush

METHOD

- Combine the dry pigments and soak them in the thinner overnight. Grind the mixture with the back of a teaspoon to create a smooth, lump-free paste. Transfer the varnish to a sealable glass jar and add the prepared pigment. Stir thoroughly.

- Do not prime wood, but before application make sure it is clean and dry. In a well-ventilated room apply the stain with a brush, working it into the wood where necessary. Apply one coat only for interior use and three coats for weatherproof protection of exterior wood. Let each coat dry thoroughly before applying the next.

SAFETY: always wear a dust mask when handling pigments and follow safety instructions when working with oil-based products

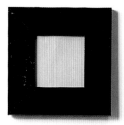

casein milk paint

beeswax

IVORY DISTRESSED FINISH

This is a fun and interesting way of using casein milk paint to produce an aged-looking finish, or simply an unusual, silky textured finish. Suitable for furniture, picture frames, and all wooden surfaces.

INGREDIENTS

Coverage: approximately 3yds² (2.5m²)

- *sandpaper*
- *½lb (.25kg) casein milk paint (distemper)*
- *approximately 1 cup (.25 liter) water*
- *clean plastic container with lid*
- *spoon*
- *small to medium-sized brush*
- *steel wool*
- *¼lb (.1kg) beeswax-based furniture wax*
- *rag*

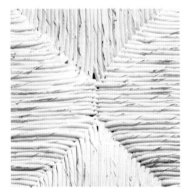

METHOD

■ Sand the surface to provide a good key. Put the powdered casein milk paint into a sealable plastic container and add water, while stirring slowly, until the paint has a pastelike consistency (or "porridge without the lumps" as it has been phrased). The paint should not drip or run, but adhere well to the surface.

■ In a cool, ventilated room apply the paint with a small to medium-sized brush. The translucent milk paint becomes opaque as it dries. Allow one coat to dry completely before applying another.

■ When the second coat has completely dried use steel wool to gently rub the surface, producing a subtle sheen similar to eggshell. Apply furniture wax with some steel wool and polish with a rag.

■ If a distressed effect is desired, lightly sand the edges of your piece before waxing to reveal the original finish underneath.

GRAY WOOD STAIN

This stain can be used to lighten new or old pine floors or other wooden surfaces, giving them a lovely driftwood look. Finish with wax or varnish depending on how hard-wearing the effect needs to be.

INGREDIENTS

Coverage: approximately 12–24yds^2 (10–20m^2)

- ¾–1oz (20–30g) zinc white pigment
- ¾–1oz (20–30g) black iron oxide pigment
- ⅔ cup (.2 liter) turpentine or thinner
- glass jar
- teaspoon
- 1 quart (1 liter) linseed oil varnish
- large glass jar with lid
- spoon
- brush

METHOD

■ Soak the pigments separately in jars with enough thinner to cover overnight. Grind the mixtures with the backs of teaspoons to create smooth, lump-free pastes. Pour the varnish into a sealable glass jar and add the prepared pigments. Stir thoroughly.

■ Do not prime wood, but before application make sure it is clean and dry. In a well-ventilated room apply the stain with a brush, working it into the wood where necessary. Apply one coat only and leave to dry thoroughly.

SAFETY: *always wear a dust mask when handling pigments and follow safety instructions when working with oil-based products*

zinc white

black iron oxide

CHECKERBOARD FINISH

This is a lovely finish for wooden floors because it leaves the grain visible. Protect the floor with floor wax or varnish. You can also adapt this effect for a wall by using two contrasting colors.

INGREDIENTS

Coverage: approximately 12–24yds² (10–20m²)

- *3 cups (0.75 liter) gray wood stain (adapt recipe on p. 134)*
- *brush*
- *1¾ cups (0.4 liter) ebony wood stain (see p. 130)*
- *paint tray*
- *hardboard square cut to appropriate size*
- *sponge square cut to the same size as the hardboard*
- *small piece of wood, to use as a handle*
- *glue*

METHOD

■ In a well-ventilated room apply the white wood stain all over the floor. Leave to dry thoroughly. Prepare the ebony wood stain and transfer it to a paint tray.

■ Measure your floor to ascertain the size you would like the squares of the pattern to be and draw a pencil grid on the flow to use as a guide. Cut some plywood and a sponge to size of square needed and glue the sponge to the wood. Glue a small piece of wood to the back of the plywood to act as a handle.

■ Dab the stamp into the ebony stain and practice applying it on some paper. Use the pencil grid to guide you as you stamp the floor. Leave to thoroughly dry. To soften the checked effect, thin down some more gray wood stain with turpentine or citrus peel thinner and apply all over the floor.

SAFETY: always follow safety instructions when working with oil-based products

healing with black and white

BLACK AND WHITE IN FENG SHUI

Black and white have strongly contrasting roles in the practice of feng shui. Black is associated with the water element and can therefore be a great source of inspiration. Yet it is also incredibly powerful and must be used sparingly to avoid encouraging feelings of oppression. Instead of introducing large areas of black, try activating its positive aspects by introducing water, a collection of glass objects or anything with a wavy shape reminiscent of this element. White, on the other hand, is linked to metal and brings with it qualities of leadership and creativity. It also stands

BELOW White rooms can be contemplative and creative; black, on the other hand, can easily become overwhelming and should be used sparingly in home interiors.

White rooms foster purity yet have naturally low energy levels.

Placing something brightly colored on a white wall—a painting, for example—helps the energy to flow again.

A wavy-shaped lamp will introduce the water element into a room.

Large expanses of black should be avoided; instead, use it in smaller areas where it will be inspirational rather than oppressive.

for purity, and is believed to have strong links with children. The inherent energy of white, however, is quite low, which means that a room with plain white walls could easily become stagnant. To alleviate this, place something vibrant or colorful against the backdrop as an alternative focus.

BLACK AND WHITE
IN COLOR THERAPY

Black and white do not correspond to a particular area or function of the body. However, they do have a profound effect on our emotions.

Because it is an enclosing color, black or deep gray surroundings can make you feel protected and secure. However, if you are prone to depression, they will exacerbate negativity.

White, on the other hand, encourages a sense of peace and purity, bringing about deep cleansing on a physical, emotional, and spiritual level. A white room will encourage you to think clearly and without limitations, though in some cases its coldness could also bring about a sense of isolation.

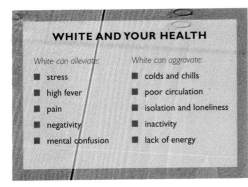

WHITE AND YOUR HEALTH

White can alleviate:
- stress
- high fever
- pain
- negativity
- mental confusion

White can aggravate:
- colds and chills
- poor circulation
- isolation and loneliness
- inactivity
- lack of energy

real life

Black and white are not necessarily easy to use—you have to avoid creating an environment that merely looks boring, rather than restfully sophisticated. White is often most successful in a room enhanced by good natural light—sunshine flooding in will create a haven with Mediterranean appeal.

HALLWAYS are often busy spaces, but feng shui (and common sense) states that it is far healthier if these central areas of the house are kept simple and clear. A white color scheme effortlessly achieves this sense of freedom and provides a refreshing contrast to the rooms that open off of it—providing you resist the temptation to cover the walls with pictures or fill space with furniture.

As a change from brilliant white, try using warm creamy-whites or misty gray-whites.

THIS STRIKING SCHEME plays with perspective in a stairwell. Gray—which is, of course, a combination of black and white—striped wallpaper

Well-chosen ceramics will enhance a monochrome scheme and prevent it from appearing stark or austere.

is cleverly hung both vertically and horizontally in order to draw the eye first across to the doorway and then down from the ceiling. The whole monochrome effect is enhanced by the introduction of a shelf of ceramics whose shapes and patterns accentuate the vertical movement and whose color is strictly monochrome. The resulting still-life shows how, even in the absence of bright color, black-and-white rooms can create just as much interest by playing with variations in form, line, and tone.

Touches of green—a vase of flowers or a plant with striking foliage—give a fresh accent to all-white schemes.

THIS BEDROOM is restful, relaxing, and conducive to the most peaceful night's sleep. Creating an all-white room takes courage, and maintaining one requires more than a little discipline, but you may well feel that the results are so striking that it is worth sacrificing clutter, bright color, and pattern in at least one room in the house. Choose somewhere that gets plenty of natural light, because this will enhance the sun-bleached effect, and opt for paint that is a warm, milky white instead of a brilliant blue-white, to ensure that the room never feels cold. A touch of greenery, as displayed in the unusual wall vases shown here, fits perfectly with the naturalistic theme.

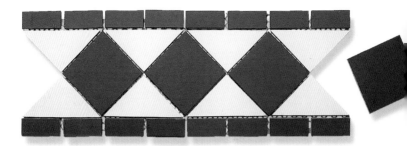

THE CLASSIC and familiar combination of black and white is used here to create clean, simple lines, perfect for a fitted kitchen. The juxtaposition of sleek black tiles and plain white cupboards creates a dramatically modernist effect and makes this strictly monochrome room scheme seem somewhat masculine and functional. But these unbroken blocks of color are cleverly counterbalanced by the checkerboard floor—a time-honored pattern using small black inset tiles—which softens the contrasts elsewhere in the room, and introduces a more traditional note to the overall effect.

Black-and-white floor tiles have formed striking color contrasts in home interiors for years. As a variation on the favorite checkerboard pattern, consider installing a monochrome border around the edge of the room.

good combinations

Together, black and white form the strongest of contrasts. Because black is receding and white is advancing, when combined they play games with perspective. So use the two together when you want to create maximum visual impact and simple sophistication—for example, on a checkerboard floor, in an art deco bathroom, or as part of a dramatic modern scheme.

Combined with rich creams and golds, black becomes opulent and sophisticated; matched with deep reds it is quintessential chinoiserie; when married with greens it is intense and masculine. Avoid using black alongside yellow, a juxtaposition that always appears alarming, and beware of how it interacts with blues and purples, which can easily seem dull and muddy in comparison.

White is altogether easier to handle because it has the advantage of combining successfully with any color in the spectrum. It will give an instant lift in many circumstances, breaking up an expanse of color, cooling down hot shades of red, orange, or yellow, enhancing the intensity of blues, freshening greens, brightening purples, and cleansing neutrals. It is good in low levels of natural light and in confined areas, where it gives the illusion of brightness and space, but it also enhances the sun-drenched appeal of naturally airy rooms.

Designers use the simple combination of black and white to striking effect.

The pairing of black or deep gray with a strong, bright red adds an Asian flair.

A fresh, bright color, such as lime green, combines well with a cool gray background shade.

Whites and creams always work well beside shades of blue.

Black and yellow is a jolting mix; gray and primrose is altogether easier on the eye.

Gentle shades of mossy green or blue sit happily with cool grays..

Brash lime green and dove grey combine in this simple yet refreshing room

tone and texture

Black, white, and gray are easy to coordinate —whatever you place together, nothing will clash. But make up for the lack of bright color by varying texture and tone: place rough next to smooth, light beside dark, refined against rough-hewn. The more you include, the more interesting the result.

neutrals

THERE is something incredibly restful and uncomplicated about neutral colors—from ivory and buff to mushroom and chestnut—because they are all borrowed from the natural world around us. Bringing them into your home, either by using plenty of raw materials such as wood, stone, and wicker, or by painting your walls in similar tones, will give a harmonious look that can be earthy or elegant, subtle or striking.

inspirations

For years, rich, glowing primary colors were the preserve of the wealthy, while neutrals were linked with simple, country interiors. This was because the earth pigments from which the neutral pigments were derived were inexpensive and plentiful. Neutral colors have kept their associations with uncomplicated style ever since, though some shades of brown and cream have enjoyed popularity among the wealthy at various times in the past. Cream, for example, had its heyday in the 18th century, while brown paint was ubiquitous in stylish Victorian parlors.

This ability to create a range of looks from the blissfully simple to the devastatingly sophisticated, makes neutrals one of the most versatile color families available to the interior designer. It is, however, important to decide in advance which look you prefer—the rustic or the refined. Much will depend on what inspired you in the first place. A stoneware pitcher, a fossil ammonite, or a piece of driftwood would lead to the room having a wonderfully down-to-earth feel. A collection of cream colored pottery, an elegant stone statue, or a fine cashmere throw would give rise to an altogether smarter look.

A walk in the woods, across some fields, along a beach, or even a stroll

A beachcombing expedition might unearth a collection of driftwood whose salt-bleached colors and diverse textures could find their way onto a decorator's palette.

Fossil ammonites nestle in limestone, a reminder that a range of subtle colors can be inspired by natural materials.

through the park will provide lots of inspiration for neutral schemes that you can bring into your home. At the paler end of the color family you will see shades of ivory, bone, and cream; those with a grayish tinge include taupe, mushroom, and stone. For yellow-based neutrals, look to straw, sandstone, and biscuit; if you want a shade with a hint of green, there's khaki or drab.

Nature provides us with a range of darker browns too, from glossy, red-based chestnut to the soft, gray-brown of nutmeg and tree bark. Basing your room schemes on the colors you see together in nature is the easiest way to ensure harmonious results.

This teapot's rich glaze reveals the depth and variation of color that is possible even within this limited palette.

Another key to the success of neutral rooms is to think carefully about the texture of the elements you introduce. Because the colors in the neutral palette are so closely related, some variation in texture is essential in order to provide extra visual interest. Introducing naturally rough-and-ready materials is the easiest way to do this: coir or seagrass matting, whitewashed floorboards, raw linen curtains, coarse woolen throws, rough-hewn stone flooring, and unfinished wood furniture will all contribute valuable surface pattern, as well as neutral color.

Choose furniture that is in keeping with the other neutral elements in the room.

If you feel that a neutral room needs a lift, make the most of accent colors to inject some life. Inspiration may come from a drift of poppies in a cornfield, a pretty shell in the sand, or a vivid toadstool on the forest floor.

COFFEE AND CREAM CLASSIC PAINTS

These paints will work well together in traditional, classic, or modern interiors. They act as a backdrop to architectural features, interesting pieces of furniture, and interior accessories. The colors have been selected for their versatility as backgrounds for other shades, but it is worth bearing in mind when choosing them that the pigment color should be in harmony with a feature already in the room and agreeable to you personally.

INGREDIENTS

Coverage: approximately 24–36yds^2 (20–30m^2)

Coffee paint using reddish brown pigment:

- 5¼oz (150g) brown ochre pigment
- 1 quart (1 liter) water
- glass jar
- ½ gallon (2.5 liters) white latex paint
- clean plastic bucket
- spoon
- small brush for edges
- large brush

Cream paint using yellow pigment:

- 3½oz (100g) raw sienna pigment
- 1 quart (1 liter) water
- glass jar
- ½ gallon (2.5 liters) white latex paint
- clean plastic bucket
- spoon
- small brush for edges
- large brush

METHOD

- Soak the pigment in enough water to cover overnight, ensuring any lumps are dissolved. Add the prepared pigment to the latex paint in a bucket and mix thoroughly.
- Make sure your wall is smooth and clean. In a cool, ventilated room, apply the paint systematically, using a small brush at the edges first. You will need to apply two coats, but always let the first coat dry completely before applying the next.

SAFETY: always wear a dust mask when handling pigments

GRAY AND CREAM CLASSIC PAINTS

Like coffee and cream (see pp. 150–1), these paints work well next to each other and suit any style of interior. Remember, however, that the pigment color should harmonize with something already in the room for the best effect.

INGREDIENTS

Coverage: approximately 24–36yds^2 (20–30m^2)

Light gray paint using black pigment:

- 1¾oz (50g) black iron oxide pigment
- 1 quart (1 liter) water
- glass jar
- teaspoon
- ½ gallon (2.5 liters) white latex paint
- clean plastic bucket
- spoon
- small brush for edges
- large brush

Cream paint (see *p. 150*)

METHOD

■ Soak the pigment in enough water to cover overnight. Break up any lumps using the back of a teaspoon. Add the prepared pigment to the latex paint in a bucket and stir thoroughly.

■ Before application make sure your wall surface is smooth, clean, and dust free. In a cool, well-ventilated room apply the paint systematically, using a small brush at the edges first. You will need to apply two coats, allowing the first coat to dry completely before applying the next.

SAFETY: always wear a dust mask when handling pigments

GLAZED WALL FINISH

This finish looks very effective on top of white latex paint, giving the surface a mellow, aged effect and a gloss finish that reflects the light. It is also extremely tough and washable. Ideally suited to hallways and bathrooms.

INGREDIENTS

Coverage: approximately 24yds² (20m²)

- ½ gallon (2.5 liters) white latex paint
- roller
- 1½ quarts (1.5 liters) gloss floor and yacht varnish
- large brush
- small brush for edges

METHOD

■ In a cool, ventilated room, use a roller to apply two or three coats of white latex paint, allowing each coat to dry thoroughly and ensuring the surface is entirely covered.

■ Apply gloss floor and yacht varnish with a brush, cutting in the edges carefully with a second, smaller brush. Avoid going over the surface more than once and apply the varnish carefully to reduce the risk of drips and runs. Leave to dry for at least 12 hours, during which time the surface will darken and yellow.

■ The first layer is absorbed by the paint, so apply a second layer in the same way. A third layer may be applied after drying, to strengthen the effect.

SAFETY: always follow safety instructions when using oil-based products

WHITE CRACKLE GLAZE

This finish imitates aged paintwork and is best–suited to decorative items since the effect will not withstand much handling. This recipe uses white for a neutral, tone-on-tone effect, but the crackle glaze could be applied between different-colored paints.

INGREDIENTS

Coverage: approximately 18yds² (15m²)

- *½ gallon (2.5 liters) white latex paint*
- *3 brushes*
- *1¼ cups (.3 liters) crackle glaze medium*
- *3¼ cups (.75 liters) transparent oil glaze*

SAFETY: always follow safety instructions when using oil-based products and crackle glaze medium

METHOD

■ Use a brush to paint the surface with a coat of white latex paint and leave to dry. Apply two or three coats to ensure a solid covering; this base coat will be the color that shows through the cracks.

■ Once dry, working in a well-ventilated room, carefully apply a generous layer of crackle glaze, brushing horizontally or vertically according to the direction in which you wish the cracks to appear.

■ Leave the glaze to dry following the instructions on the label, and then apply a top coat of latex paint, taking care not to cover the same area twice. The cracks will start to appear immediately. Leave to dry completely before quickly and lightly applying a layer of transparent oil glaze for protection and to give an aged look. Leave to dry overnight.

healing with neutrals

NEUTRALS IN FENG SHUI

Browns, creams, beiges, and taupes are associated with the Earth and symbolic of wholeness and unity. They have a grounding effect on a room, making those inside feel whole, secure, and at one with themselves. These shades also encourage a sense of wisdom, foster healthy relationships, and promote balanced good health. In addition to neutral colors, natural materials—wool, cotton, linen, stone, brick, earthenware—also encourage Earth energy to flow.

BELOW *Neutral colors and natural materials will ensure good emotional and physical health and renew your links with the Earth and its energy.*

Plenty of natural materials in a neutrally decorated room will encourage the flow of Earth energy.

Dining in a sunroom overlooking a garden will enhance Earth energy.

Dining rooms benefit from a palette of browns and creams because these colors bring about healthy relationships among family and friends.

Neutral schemes are good in all areas of the house, but are especially nurturing in bedrooms and dining rooms. Use neutrals when you feel there is something missing from your life—perhaps love, deep friendship, or physical well-being. Chances are that simply rebalancing the Earth energy will bring about the changes you crave.

NEUTRALS IN COLOR THERAPY

For color therapists, neutral colors act as a stabilizing influence in the home. They are useful in cases where a person suffers from low self-esteem or has a tendency to overanalyze things. In some people, however, dark brown can bring about a sense of emotional stagnation—if this is a danger, opt for lighter neutrals and add accents of red or violet.

Any room in the house can benefit from the earthiness of this color palette. Against such a neutral backdrop you can add splashes of healing colors as and when you need them—perhaps a rug, a painting, a cushion, or some flowers—changing them later according to your developing needs.

NEUTRALS AND YOUR HEALTH

Neutrals can alleviate:
- low self-esteem
- overactive mind
- vulnerability
- anxiety
- relationship problems

Neutrals can aggravate:
- trapped emotions
- insularity
- lack of willpower
- sluggish thinking
- indifference

real life

Neutrals are the perfect backdrop to rustic, back-to-nature schemes that make great use of texture—from a variety of woods to coir matting, antique lace, crisp cotton, and nubby weaves. Get rid of unnecessary clutter and enjoy the relaxed simplicity that can be achieved with a palette of naturalistic, neutral colors.

This cool, neutral herringbone woodblock flooring adds a touch of sophistication to this simple setting.

THIS IS a more modern take on the simply decorated kitchen, yet the neutral color scheme is still vital in maintaining its cool and convivial atmosphere. Off-white walls, a limed herringbone wood-block floor, a bleached table and benches, and monochrome accessories are essential ingredients, leaving plenty of space for working, eating, and socializing in a relaxed fashion.

Keep kitchen color schemes simple to maintain a fresh and convivial atmosphere. Neutral colors create a sense of space even in small rooms.

A NEUTRAL color scheme is perfect for high-traffic rooms such as kitchens, because their decor provides an unfussy backdrop that calms rather than contributes to the excitement. A scrubbed pine refectory table and bare wooden chairs are practical choices that are very much in keeping with this uncomplicated, natural approach since their subtle, natural color variations are in harmony with the surrounding surfaces. Add plain glassware and sturdy china, and you have the perfect family kitchen.

Add bare wooden accessories to neutral room schemes; they are simple and natural, and blend in well with the uncomplicated style that is the hallmark of these understated interiors.

THERE'S A FUNCTIONAL yet comfortable appearance to this uncomplicated bathroom, and its neutral-colored walls are an integral part of the plan. Perfectly in keeping with its no-frills approach, the cream paint on the walls is as unaffected as the simple duckboard flooring, traditional shower-rose, utilitarian elongated sink, plain mirror, rustic towel basket, and galvanized laundry can. It is, however, a rich enough shade to make the room feel warm—an important consideration given that it is quite spacious and could otherwise appear somewhat lofty and unwelcoming.

Natural sponges, pumices, loofahs, and basketware would make perfect all-natural acessories for a down-to-earth bathroom.

SIMPLE STONE-colored neutrals inspired the decorative scheme in this living room, which has deliberately been kept as simple and unadorned as possible. The walls are painted in a tone that matches both the natural flooring and the oatmeal-colored upholstery fabric on the sofa and chairs, but they all have subtly differing surface textures to compensate for the uniformity in color. Pure white woodwork and a plain tablelamp form a crisp contrast to the muddier shades seen elsewhere in the room, making such a restrained scheme surprisingly refreshing.

A certain amount of variation in both texture and pattern is essential in neutrally decorated rooms.

Lighting doesn't have to be high-tech: for simple, natural schemes choose wooden fittings with paper shades.

good combinations

As a rule, all neutrals combine well with each other —a fact that makes this color family particularly easy to manipulate. You needn't worry about looking for the right shade of neutral paint to match a porridge-colored carpet, for example, since any shade from the palest cream to the coolest stone is likely to blend well. If you combine shiny surfaces with matte, rough with smooth, sheer with uneven, then the variation in color will simply add to the richness of your scheme.

Accent colors are all-important in neutral room schemes. Here, splashes of blue instantly attract the eye.

Another way to ensure that neutral surroundings never end up plain and boring is to introduce an accent color somewhere in the room. Choose a vase, a throw, or a cushion cover in an entirely different color—perhaps lime green, deep red, shocking pink, or azure blue—and set it against your neutral backdrop. It will display a glowing intensity but will never take over the room. If you are keen to experiment with bright, exciting shades, a neutral room is the perfect environment in which to put your newfound passion for color to the test.

Combine shades of porridge, dove, and stone
for the most subtle effects in neutral rooms.

Accents of shocking pink work well against
the simplest of backdrops.

Neutral shades—mushroom and chestnut,
for example—will always combine easily.

Indulge your passion for bright colors by adding
accessories that can be changed when required.

Neutrals will take the heat out of fiery shades
of orange and red.

This pale olive backdrop allows the hot pink
accent color to sing out without dominating.

pale and interesting

Use the palest neutrals as an alternative to white
on areas such as woodwork and ceilings.
Ivory or cream will give a softer effect
than white and, though just as amenable
next to other colors, they will give the finished
room a touch more sophistication.

metallics

METALLIC paints add glittering and eye-catching interest to all types of decorative schemes, even when used on a small scale—perhaps a gilded architrave, a pewter fire screen, or a verdigris frame. These rarefied and unusual finishes complement a huge range of colors, lifting them and adding unparalleled depth and richness. From silver and gold to bronze and copper, these are the finishing touches that will highlight the rich hues in your colorful home.

inspirations

Metallic finishes are currently enjoying something of a revival, and inspiration is coming from many different sources ranging from salvage yards to stately homes. The growing range of metallic paints and powders can be used to add either a timeworn patina or a sense of grandeur to anything from moldings, architraves, and staircases to door handles, light fittings, and furniture. Don't forget, though, that metallic finishes can also work successfully on a larger scale in home interiors; many subtle metallic paint finishes are designed to give a wonderful shine to an entire expanse of wall.

On a smaller scale, metallic objects around your home may well spark off a stream of ideas. For example, you may decide to emulate the finish of a verdigris candlestick on some nearby paneling or trim or to pick up the coppery tones of an old kettle and transfer them to the handles and drawer pulls of your kitchen cabinets.

From cool steel to warm brass, there's a wealth of metallics to choose from.

Light interacts with metallic surfaces in wonderful ways, so plan a room's lighting so that reflections are enhancing rather than intrusive, steel, silver, gold or brass will add sparkle to an interior.

Alternatively, the aged look of some fire irons could perhaps be the inspirational starting point for a metal-effect fire screen; alternatively a small cluster of picture frames could be painted a shade of silver to match a decorative metallic lamp base that stands alongside. Similarly, a bronze statue could inspire the metallic finish applied to your room's architectural detailing, or a gilt-edged mirror could be the inspiration for accentuating a gold colorwash on a whole wall.

Visit stately homes and see how metallics can heighten the sense of grandeur. Notice how your eye is drawn to gilded picture frames or how a cabinet filled with lusterware gives depth to a display of ceramics.

Old-fashioned kitchen utensils bring metallic surfaces into everyday use—think stove-top kettles, copper pans, and blackened iron grates.

Your inspiration may also come from outdoors too: a piece of fool's gold you once found on a beachcombing expedition, a rusty table and chairs that are sitting at the bottom of the garden, or some wrought-iron railings decorating a balcony.

The materials themselves may also inspire you: gilded detailing can be achieved with Dutch metal leaf or gold paint, which are all more affordable options than traditional real gold leaf. Silver paint can be used to give a cooler sheen, while a huge choice of metallic powders ranges from bronze and copper to sleek aluminum and burnished iron.

Fabrics woven with gold thread or printed with metallic designs can be used for curtains, upholstery, cushions, and throws, while reflective wallcoverings, mirrors, and shiny tiles also produce that distinctive metallic glitter. Use these finishes either to add a touch of opulence to your surroundings or to create a high-tech look.

Golden hues will add richness and joy to your surroundings.

latex glazing liquid gold powder

GOLD COLORWASH

*A gold colorwash on top of other vibrant colors like
the **Victorian Green Paint** (see pp. 72–3) or the **Ultramarine Violet
Casein** (see pp. 114–5) can lend a beautiful rich warmth to
a cold or stark scheme, and is surprisingly easy to apply.*

INGREDIENTS

Coverage: approximately 36–48yds^2
(30–40m^2)

- *2 cups (.5 liters) clear latex glazing liquid*
- *2oz (60g) gold metallic powder*
- *1 quart (1 liter) water*
- *clean plastic bucket*
- *spoon*
- *brush*

METHOD

■ Add the gold metallic powder to the latex glazing liquid in a bucket and add the water. Stir thoroughly until all the ingredients are well blended.

■ In a cool, ventilated room, practice applying your wash with a brush, using free, rhythmic movements, in an unobtrusive area or on some paper. Then apply the wash to the walls, finishing one wall at a time before moving on. Because the gold tends to swim to the surface, keep your gold colorwash well-stirred during application.

SAFETY: always wear a dust mask when handling metallic powders

METALLIC STIPPLE

The metallic stipple emulates the look of stone and minerals if applied over a classic neutral paint (see pp. 150–3). Also suitable for application over other colors and finishes, metallic stipple adds interest to any item of furniture or accessory.

INGREDIENTS

Coverage: approximately 24yds² (20m²)

- ⅓ cup (.1 liter) clear latex glazing liquid
- ¼oz (7g) bronze glimmer metallic powder
- 2 cups (0.5 liters) water
- clean plastic bucket
- spoon
- brush
- rag
- stippling brush

METHOD

■ Add the bronze glimmer metallic powder to the latex glazing liquid in a bucket and add the water. Stir thoroughly until all the ingredients are well-blended.

■ In a ventilated room, practice applying the mixture with a brush, using smooth movements, in an unobtrusive place on your surface or on some paper. Apply the colorwash very quickly to ensure it does not dry out. Lift off any brush marks with a rag. Keep stirring the solution during application because it tends to separate.

■ Lightly dab the stippling brush into the still-wet colorwash all over the surface. Change the angle of the stippling brush to vary the effect. Tackle one section of the wall at a time for the best results.

SAFETY: always wear a dust mask when handling metallic powders

yellow ochre white latex paint gold powder

GOLD-OCHRE WASH

This is a luxurious and beautiful combination suitable for the decoration of a special dining room or living room. The effect of the gold is subtle and would be best enhanced by daylight in a south- or west-facing room or by uplighters and candles at night. A good base for this effect is a wall painted in a similar color or lined with paper.

INGREDIENTS

Coverage: approximately 48yds² (40m²)

- 9oz (250g) yellow ochre pigment
- glass jar
- 1 quart (1 liter) water
- teaspoon
- 5¼ quarts (5 liters) white latex paint
- 5¼oz (150g) gold metallic powder
- small brush for edges
- large brush
- bucket

METHOD

■ Soak the pigment in enough water to cover overnight. Break up any lumps using the back of a teaspoon. Add the prepared pigment and the gold metallic powder to the latex paint in a bucket. Stir thoroughly. Add some water to your mix if the paint is unwieldy.

■ Make sure the walls are smooth, clean, and dust free. In a cool, ventilated room, apply the paint systematically, using the small brush at the edges first. You might need to apply two coats, but always let the first coat dry completely before applying a further one. Stir the solution during application because it frequently tends to separate.

SAFETY: always wear a dust mask when handling pigments and metallic powders

linseed oil varnish

silver powder

SILVER STARDUST PAINT

This recipe makes a small quantity of silver paint that looks stunning on top of black, dark blue, or dark red surfaces. The paint is suitable for the decoration of small ornamental accessories but not objects that are handled regularly.

INGREDIENTS

Coverage: approximately 6yds² (5m²)

- *sandpaper*
- *½ cup (.125 liters) linseed oil varnish*
- *2tsps silver metallic powder*
- *large glass jar with lid*
- *spoon*
- *brush*
- *rag (optional)*

METHOD

■ Lightly sand the surface to provide a good key. Pour the varnish into a sealable glass jar and add the silver metallic powder, stirring thoroughly. Keep stirring the paint as you work to prevent the powder from settling.

■ In a cool, ventilated room, practice your application technique in an unobtrusive area applying the paint thickly. Paint the object by covering the whole surface or dabbing the paint on thickly with a rag. Leave to dry overnight.

SAFETY: always wear a dust mask when handling metallic powders and follow safety instructions when working with oil-based products

healing with metallics

BELOW *The stabilizing nature of metal means that a traditional kitchen, complete with iron stove, copper kettle, and fire-blackened pans, is filled with its energy.*

METALLICS IN FENG SHUI

Metal energy has special qualities that make its presence in the home comforting and stabilizing. It inspires creativity, symbolizes ripening and fruition, makes people feel secure and joyful, and represents sound financial reward. Placing objects around you that are made of steel, silver, brass, copper, or iron will intensify these properties, especially if these items are curved, rounded, arched, or domed—shapes that have a particular association with this element.

The presence of metal in your surroundings also speeds up the flow of energy in a room. So if you sense that

Dome-shaped objects are associated with the Metal element.

Energy can become stagnant in the corner of a room—encourage it to flow with decorative metal objects.

Natural flooring such as cork will provide a counterbalance to the presence of metal.

an area of your house has an energy block or stagnation, introducing objects such as bronze statues, pewter boxes, or metal wind chimes, or even covering a whole wall with a metallic paint effect, is likely to help. Bear in mind, though, that too many metal objects can make a room feel cold and clinical. If so, restore the balance by adding some natural materials, richly textured fabrics, or soft furnishings.

METALLICS IN COLOR THERAPY

Color therapy associates gold with a wealth of knowledge, refinement, and understanding. It is linked to the power of the sun, and so brings life and energy. Silver, on the other hand, represents the moon, which is soothing, cooling, purifying, and balancing. Visualizing gold during meditation is a profound way to heal the body and boost it with new life, while filling the mind's eye with silver is deeply cleansing. These qualities are the basis of yogic breathing exercises that encourage you to imagine that you are inhaling golden light and exhaling cool silver light.

METALLICS AND YOUR HEALTH

Silver can alleviate:	*Silver can aggravate:*
■ fear and negativity	■ excessive heat
■ lack of understanding	■ physical or mental
■ lack of energy	imbalance
■ healing	■ hyperactivity
■ mental strain	■ toxicity
	■ inflexibility

real life

Metallics can supply a hard-edged, modern look. The reflective quality of metal will also provide a more traditional appeal by contributing soft glints, especially where combined with firelight.

AN EXPANSE OF METAL gives a professional edge to this minimalist kitchen. Wonderfully slick stainless steel is a practical and aesthetically pleasing choice, not only for the cabinets but also for everything from the oven, stove, and extractor hood to pans, toaster, kettle, and storage jars. With dark granite work-surfaces and splashbacks, and little extra adornment or clutter, the pale wood flooring injects essential natural warmth and color variation into this calm and efficient workspace.

This Alessi design classic would perfectly complement a streamlined, designer kitchen, further enriching the range of metallic surfaces on view.

THIS HIGH-TECH mix of metal and glass could feel cold and clinical, yet thanks to the free-flowing curves of the basin, mirror, and faucet it becomes organic and user-friendly. The simple white walls and monochrome accessories mean that there is no bright color distracting the eye in this bathroom; the decorating emphasis and visual interest are therefore provided exclusively by the sheen of the metal, the repetition of circles seen against squares, and the texture of the glass.

Metallic accessories enhance the clean, simple lines of a bathroom. Choose shiny finishes for a sleek look; matte surfaces for a softer effect.

 METALLIC SURFACES bring life and sparkle to a room; as the eye is drawn to them, they become its decorative focus. But to followers of feng shui, metal objects are also thought to increase the flow of beneficial energy. Round, curved, or spherical shapes are particularly auspicious because they encourage the positive qualities associated with this element—leadership, solid family values, and security. This attractive display of antique copper pots and pans, burnished and worn from decades of constant use, adds an element of warmth and antiquity to what might otherwise be a somewhat cold and clinical kitchen. Their arrangement against a neutral background adds to the character of the room.

Warm metallic tones can be introduced by incorporating copper, brass, or gold leaf into a room scheme.

A **METALLIC-FINISH** curtain and a modern tubular metal chair deliver cooling, silvery shades to a quiet corner of a bedroom. This futuristic decor makes this area a perfect place to sit and rest. Color theorists tell us that the proliferation of metallic surfaces are cooling, cleansing, harmonizing, and calming —qualities associated with silver in healing environments such as color therapy and yogic relaxation exercises.

Despite the presence of so much metal, this room proves that metallic schemes need not be cold or distant; this scheme has an unexpected gentleness and warmth thanks to an arrangement of flowers and the gently flowing folds of the fabric.

Clean lines and clinical metal are combined to stunning effect in this desk lamp designed by Philippe Starck.

good combinations

Golden finishes complement strong colors such as vermilion, sapphire, and emerald, creating an affect that is reminiscent of glowing medieval illuminated manuscripts. The richness of all these hues is enhanced by the warmth of gilding: visualize the effects that can be created by stenciling gold stars onto a royal blue wall, sewing old-gold braid onto a plum-colored damask tablecloth or adding a golden colorwash to a forest green wall. Yet gold can also inject vitality into the subtlest of color schemes: imagine how a pale green wall would be made richer with the addition of a touch of gilding on the chair rail; or picture a powder blue room warmed by a gold-framed mirror.

The best color partners for silver finishes are shades such as sugar pink, lilac, and navy, which complement the coolness of the metal. Meanwhile, copper has a natural affinity with green, iron with monochrome schemes, and steel with clinical white. Use metals in this way to enhance a color's coolness, warmth, richness, or simplicity and the results will be simply stunning.

Cool metal surfaces are complemented by muted pinks, lilacs, and purples, while adding a sweep of yellow alongside adds welcome warmth.

A simple gold colorwash adds warmth to the neutral and aqua tones in this scheme.

Here, the gold cushions provide an accent color to complement the hot red of the sofa.

Silver accessories mix perfectly with a classic navy-and-white regime.

Silver cushions combine with a cool lilac wall to take the heat out of this deep purple sofa.

Copper picture frames and accessories add warmth and interest to this neutral scheme.

Khaki walls and copper cushion covers combine perfectly in this unusual pairing.

metal magic

You could make the most of metallic combinations by hanging a silver-framed mirror against a deep blue wall; painting a shimmering glaze over rose-colored paint; hanging lavender voile from a wrought-iron curtain rod; or creating a kitchen with steel worktops and white walls.

index

list of resources

ACROSS CANADA
Benjamin Moore
Tel. 800-304-0304
for retailers
www.benjaminmoore.com

Pratt and
Lambert Paints
available across Canada
800-289-7728

CIL Paints
(available at independent
dealers across Canada,
Beaver Lumber and Home
Depot stores)
Tel. 800-DURABLE
for retailers

Lewiscraft
Tel. (416) 291-8406
for information

Para Paints
Tel. 800-461-PARA
for retailers

Selectone Paints
Tel. 800-875-9935

THROUGHOUT
WESTERN CANADA
Crafts Canada
Tel. (403) 219-0333
for information

General Paint
Tel. (604) 253-3131
for information
www.generalpaint.com

(BRITISH COLUMBIA)
Ashley House
Wallcoverings Inc.
1838 West Broadway
Vancouver, BC
V6J 1Y9
Tel. (604) 734-4131

By Product Fabrics
Dream Designs
956 Commercial Drive
Vancouver, BC
V5L 3W7
Tel. (604) 254-5012

Chintz and Company
950 Homer Street
Vancouver, BC
V6B 2W7
Tel. (604) 689-2022
&
1720 Store Street
Victoria, BC
V8W 1V5
Tel. (250) 381-2404

Hartmann and Brown
241 Selby Str
Nanaimo, BC
V9R 2R2
Tel. 800-665-2833

Jordans Interiors
1470 West Broadway
Vancouver, BC
V6H 1H4
Tel. (604) 733-1174
&
1539 United Boulevard
Coquitlam, BC
V3K 6Y7
Tel. (604) 522-9855

Lightheart and Company
100-535-Howe St
Vancouver, BC
V6C 1M9
Tel. (604) 684-4711

Livingspace Interiors
1550 Marine Drive
North Vancouver, BC
V7P 1T7
Tel. (604) 987-2253
&
1100 Mainland St
Vancouver, BC
V6B 2T9
Tel. (604) 683-1116

Pacific Linens
Capilano Mall
935 Marine Drive
North Vancouver, BC
V7P 1S3
Tel. (604) 980-8922
locations across Canada

Paint Inspirations
2003 West 4th Ave
Vancouver, BC
V6J 1N3
Tel. (604) 737-8558

Robin Kay Home
and Style
1670 Cypress St
Vancouver, BC
Tel. (604) 731-1199
&
1571 Marine Drive
West Vancouver, BC
V7V 1H9
Tel. (604) 925-6611
locations across Canada

Valerianne of Vancouver
3109 Granville St
Vancouver, BC
V6H 5K1
Tel. (604) 732-9646

World Mosaic
1665 West 7th Avenue
Vancouver, BC
V6J 1S4
Tel. (604) 736-8158

(**ALBERTA**)
Chintz and Company
1238 11th Ave SW
Calgary, AB
T3C 0M4
Tel. (403) 245-3449
&
10502 105th Ave NW
Edmonton, AB
T5H 0K8
Tel. (403) 428-8181

Day's Painting Supplies
10733 104 Ave. N.W.
Edmonton, AB
T5J 3K1
Tel. (780) 426-4848

Walls Alive
1328 17th Ave S.W.
Calgary, AB
T2T 0C3
Tel. (403) 244-8931

**EASTERN CANADA
(ONTARIO)**
Elte Carpet and Home
80 Ronald Ave
Toronto, ON
M6E 5A2
Tel. (416) 785-1225

**Ontario Paint
and Wallpaper**
1275 Queen St East
Toronto, ON
M5A 1S6
Tel. (416) 362-5127

**Primavera Interior
Furnishings Ltd.**
160 Tears Ave,
Suite 110
Toronto, Ontario
M5R 3P8
Tel. (416) 921-3334

Country Floors
321 Davenport Road
Toronto, Ontario
M5R 1K5
Tel. (416) 922-9214

Au Lit Fine Linens
630 Mount Pleasant Road
Toronto, Ontario
M4S 2N1
Tel. (416) 488-9662

Cruikshank's
780 Birchmount Road,
Unit 16 Toronto, Ontario
M1K 5H4
Tel. (416) 750-9249

Divine Decor
4133 Dundas St. W
Etobicoke, Ontario
M8X 1X2
Tel. (416) 236-7356

Du Verre
280 Queen Street W
Toronto, Ontario
M5V 2A1
888-DU VERRE
(388-3773)

Ethan Allen Home Interiors
Stores located in
Coquitlam, Calgary,
Edmonton, and two
in Ontario
800-228-9229
for information
Head Office: Tel.
(203) 743-8000

Pier 1 Imports
22113 Yonge St
Toronto, Ontario
M5B 1M4
Tel. (416) 363-2131
locations across Canada
800-447-4371
for information

Scantrade International
60 Horner Ave
Toronto, Ontario
M8Z 4X3
Tel. (416) 259-1127

Tower Paint
(a Division of
Cloverdale Paint Inc.)
Tel. (780) 451-3830

**Color Your World
Color Palette
(ICI Paints Canada)**

Color Your World Color
Palette paints are stocked
in many home decoration
stores. Please phone
1-800-299-9940 for details
of your nearest supplier.

acknowledgements

The publisher would like to thank the following for their generous assistance with the text, props and photography:

Paul and Pauline Allen
  for setting up and painting the sets;

Bright Ideas, Lewes;

Cargo Home Shop, Brighton;

James Emmerson
  for organising the props;

Fired Earth, Adderbury, Oxfordshire;

Furniture 151, Lewes;

Habitat, Brighton;

Lorraine Harrison for styling the sets;

ICI Paints, particularly Daryl Fryer;

Kings Framers, Lewes;

Kay MacMullan for organising the props;

Natural Fabric Company, Hungerford;

Nutshells Natural Paints, particularly
  Eilla Goldhahn and Juliet Robertson,
  for providing pigments and advice on
  the recipes;

Paint Magic, Brighton;

The Pier, Brighton.

Photography

All photography by Guy Ryecart
except the following:

Abode, UK: pps10BR, 43T, 61T,
  100B&T, 143B, 180B, 181T&M

The Bridgeman Art Library, London:
  pps49T (Phillips Collection, Washington),
  109B (Gavin Graham Library), 129B

Houses and Interiors: 62T, 120B&T
  Mark Bolton, p6
  Simon Butcher, p142R
  Verne, pps10BL, 42, 160B&T, 161

The Image Bank, London: pps28M,
  29B, 48B, 49B, 68T, 69B, 89

The Interior Archive:
  Jacques Dirand, p82TR
  Cecilia Innes, pps122B, 123T, 162T&M
  Simon McBride, pps80B&T, 81T
  G Pilkington, p101T
  Simon Upton, pps40B, 83T
  Henry Wilson, pps102B&T, 103
  Andrew Wood, pps140B, 141T&M, 163BL
  YPMA, pps42T&M, 44B

The Stock Market, London: pps109T,
  124B, 148B

Tony Stone Associates: pps29T, 69T,
  128B, 129T, 169B

Elizabeth Whiting & Associates: pps60B,
  121T, 181BR, 182B, T&M, 183B

colour
swatches

THE swatches on the following pages are coded according to the Color Your World Color Palette (see p. 191 for stockists). Use them to match paints to fabrics, flooring or interior details, or as a mix-and-match system to play with possible colour mixes. Each swatch has its corresponding paint code marked on the back and there is also a colour reference at the side of the page. The metallic tabs show inspirational colours you might choose to highlight with metallic detail.

__Note__ In order to illustrate a full range of greys, some of the shades shown on that page are designated by Pantone numbers. Pantones are a universal system for denoting colour.